JUST CALL
ME AN ANGEL

A Novel

Dan Yates

Covenant

Covenant Communications, Inc.

ACKNOWLEDGMENTS

This sequel would never have been written without the suggestion and encouragement of Valerie Holladay from Covenant Communications. Thanks, Valerie. Your editing skills are also deeply appreciated.

Thanks to my family for their technical advice, for the comments that enhanced the story, and for their encouragement. Thanks to Robin for adding a major component to the story, and to Kathy for suggesting a chapter in the first book, which opened the door to the sequel.

And special thanks to my wife, Shelby Jean, for editing all my works with love—and with lots of red ink.

Published by Covenant Communications, Inc.

American Fork, Utah

Copyright © 1996 Dan Yates

Printed in the United States of America

First Printing: August 1996

01 00 99 98 97 96 95 94   10 9 8 7 6 5 4 3 2 1

ISBN 1-55503-980-4

Library of Congress Cataloging-in-Publication Data

Yates, Dan, 1934-
      Just Call Me An Angel: /Dan Yates.
              p. cm.
      Sequel to: Angels don't knock.
      Summary: Jason returns to the earth as an angel to help Bruce overcome his insecurities and marry Sam's best friend Arline.
      ISBN 1-55503-980-4
      [1. Angels--Fiction.] I. Title.
PZ7.Y2127Cal 1996
[Fic]--dc20   96-20846
                                                          CIP
                                                          AC

PROLOGUE

Life for Samantha Allen was really quite simple. She loved teaching her fifth grade school class, going shopping with her best friend Arline Wilson, feeding the ducks in Dove Park where she enjoyed taking walks, and dreaming of that special guy she had always felt would someday step into her little world. And of course, there was Bruce Vincent.

No, she wasn't exactly in love with Bruce, and he did fall a bit short of being her perfect dream man. Still, she was very fond of him. Bruce was kind, romantic, and always considerate of her feelings. Samantha felt comfortable with Bruce, and in time came to accept that she might do worse than him. Even though she didn't exactly say "yes" when he offered her the ring, she did consent to wear it with the idea of marrying him someday. A someday not too far in the distant future.

That, pretty much, was the sum and total of Samantha's life. Or so she thought, until a certain ghost named Jason Hackett walked through the wall of her apartment, declaring he was destined to meet her.

"You and I are destined for each other, Sam," Jason told her. "It's all in the contract. The problem is, the contract has a flaw in it. You see, my friend, Gus, is in charge of these kinds of contracts, and he made a bad mistake with ours. Thanks to his typo, I was born in 1926. I should have been born in 1962. That way I would have been alive at the same time as you, Sam. I could have courted you properly."

Samantha was dumbfounded. "That's the most preposterous thing I've ever heard!" she exclaimed. "How do I date a ghost? If we can't even touch, how can you claim to be courting me?"

Samantha soon learned that Jason was "dead serious" (excuse the pun) about sticking around until she realized he was telling the truth. And so she tolerated him. And then, she began to like having him around. And then, to her complete chagrin, she fell hopelessly in love with him. Still, there was no obvious way the two of them could find a life together. She lived in one dimension, and he in another.

So she decided to marry Bruce and get on with her life.

"Good-bye, Jason," Samantha said. "I love you."

* * *

Hearing her declaration of love, Gus was ready with a new contract in the blink of an eye. He gave it to her as she was waiting for the elevator. She read the contract thoroughly, then looked at Gus without speaking.

"What are ya waiting for, Sam?" he asked. "Are ya signin' it, or not?"

"No," she answered curtly.

"No?" he stammered. "What do ya mean, no? Didn't ya read what it said? You can have Jason! Isn't that what ya wanted?"

"I'm not saying I won't sign a new contract, Gus. Just not this one. I want to negotiate a few changes in it."

Gus had no choice but to give in to Samantha's demands for negotiations. Soon a revised contract was prepared. One of the provisions was the "Bruce clause."

"I want Bruce taken care of," Samantha said. "I don't want him hurt any more than necessary."

* * *

Now, more than six months have passed since the signing of the contract, and the "Bruce clause" is in danger of falling through the cracks. A computer-generated search found a likely match for Bruce in Jenice Anderson, and he was to have married her within the year. But the parties involved have missed the boat, and the higher authorities have given Gus an ultimatum: bring it to a happy conclusion or suffer the consequences.

If Gus doesn't find a way to get those involved back on track, he will face the judgment of the higher authorities, and perhaps even worse, the wrath of Samantha. In desperation, Gus calls on his old friend Jason for help. And the fun begins.

CHAPTER ONE

"NO! I won't do it! I've already spent more than twenty years playing the part of Casper, and there's no way you're getting me back down there again. You can forget it, Gus! End of discussion."

"What kinda' attitude is that, Jason," Gus pleaded desperately. "I'm in a lurch here, pal. "How can ya even think of leavin' me hangin' out ta dry, after all we've been through together?"

Jason whirled to face Gus and shook a finger in his face.

"What we've been through is no one's fault but your own! You seem to forget it was your typo that derailed destiny in the first place."

"Now calm down, Jason. It's not like yer gonna' be down there another twenty years. The higher authorities have only approved a month on this one."

"A month? Are you out of your mind? How long do you think the Paradise Palace would keep me on as head chef if I don't show up for work all next month? I love that job, Gus. I'm not about to toss it out the window to go straighten out another mess you've gotten yourself into."

Gus dropped the contract onto a pile of unorganized paperwork on his desk, then walked over to Jason and put his arm around him.

"Wasn't I the one that got ya the job in the first place? I have the problem covered. My Uncle Arnold has agreed ta fill in for ya as long as it takes."

"Your Uncle Arnold? That guy comes about as close to being a chef as you come to being an English professor."

"Trust me, I got it all worked out. Nothin' can possibly go wrong."

"Yeah, right. The last time I trusted one of your 'nothing can go wrong' schemes, you had me believing I was getting a new body. Do you know how humiliating that is for me now? I'm the laughing stock with all my friends. No one can believe I was actually gullible enough to fall for a story like that."

"Okay, so I let ya believe a little untruth for a while. I had a hard enough time gettin' destiny back where it belonged without worryin' what you might do if I told ya the whole truth. Things are different this time, pal. You know exactly what kind of trouble I'm in here. And ya know exactly what has ta be done. Otherwise . . ."

Jason stared in disgust at his old friend and wondered if Gus really knew what he was asking. A cold chill shot through him as he remembered what it was like wandering around in a dimension where no one even knew he was there. Where he couldn't open a door, change channels on a television set, or pick up the smallest object. Thoughts of returning to such a life, even for the period of one month, were loathsome. Still—if he chose not to go—what would become of Gus? And worse yet, how would Samantha feel? After all, it was her contract that had come under the shadow of this unexpected twist of fate.

* * *

Arline Wilson stood helplessly in front of her open closet. How could she have been so careless as to spill a glass of grape punch on her favorite white dress? Her blue denim skirt with the western shirt would be perfect, but she had worn it only last week. With a frustrated sigh, she searched through her clothes once more. Then something in the back of the closet caught her eye. A lump swelled in her throat as she stared at the green pants suit hanging where she had placed it nearly seven months ago. *Is it possible,* she wondered, *that more than half a year has gone by since that day?*

Even though Arline loved the outfit, she had never worn it. Just looking at it now brought back bittersweet memories of the day she bought it. It was the day she and Samantha had attended a movie, and afterward shopped at the mall. It was also the last day Arline ever saw Samantha alive.

She removed the suit from the closet and tossed it across her bed. Today, it seemed, there was little choice but to wear it. Memories and all.

As she looked at herself in the mirror, she was momentarily distracted by what she saw. She had forgotten how much she liked the outfit. Still, it did bring to mind old habits. It would be so natural to pick up the phone as she used to do and dial Samantha's number. *I'd give anything to hear Sam's voice just once more,* she thought sadly.

In a state of melancholy, Arline moved to her still unmade bed and sat down on the edge of it. *I really should take flowers to Sam's grave,* she thought. *I've never been back since the funeral. Sam was always full of life and so much fun to be with. It's hard for me to think of her as being there, in that cold casket.* Arline glanced at her watch. It was 10:00 a.m. *Two hours before I have to be at the station. I'd have plenty of time to pick up some flowers.*

Traffic that morning was much heavier than usual, and at the florist Arline had to wait while a woman ordered flowers for an elaborate wedding. As a result, it took much longer than she expected to reach the cemetery. Bringing her green Toyota to a stop, she glanced through the window and was surprised to see a stranger standing near Samantha's headstone. He was a nice-looking man who appeared to be in his mid- to late twenties. *Who can he be?* she wondered. *Samantha never kept any secrets from me. I knew all her friends and family. I'd certainly remember if she'd mentioned a man fitting his description.* She briefly considered returning later, after he was gone, but knew she would never find the time. She stepped out of her car and gathered up the arrangement of flowers.

As Arline came near, she was surprised that the stranger turned to look at her, but didn't speak. It seemed almost as if he was deliberately ignoring her.

"Did you know her?" Arline said pointedly to the man.

"Wha . . . ?!" Jason gasped. "Are you talking to me?"

Arline gave him a startled look. "Well, of course I'm talking to you. Who else would I be talking to? We're the only ones here."

"This is incredible! You can see me—and even hear what I'm saying. That's not supposed to happen."

Arline looked at him curiously. "What are you talking about? Of course I can see you."

She was certainly unprepared for what he said next.

"I know you're going to find this hard to believe, Arline, but you've been this close to me hundreds of times in the past without knowing I was there."

Arline hardly heard what he said, so surprised was she that he knew her name. *How does he know my name?* she puzzled. *There's something very strange going on here.* Then it hit her. *He's probably one of my fans.* For the past three years, Arline had been the hostess of a radio talk show. She also made live appearances at social events now and then.

That's the answer, she sighed.

"You know me from my show, don't you?" she asked. "How long have you been listening?"

"Your show? I . . . uh . . ."

"Hey, don't be embarrassed. I'm just an ordinary person like you. It's not like I'm a big celebrity," Arline said with a laugh.

"That's right," Jason responded. "You are the hostess of a radio show. I should have remembered."

"I have to admit I'm flattered," Arline said conversationally. "I can't remember affecting anyone quite like this before."

Jason's voice was peevish. "Yeah, well, you're not any more flattered than I am confused. Something strange is going on here, and I have no idea what it is."

Again Arline wondered at Jason's meaning but shrugged it off. Stepping around him, she placed her flowers near the headstone.

"I miss her so much," she said softly, pulling a tissue from her purse to wipe away the tears that glimmered in her eyes. "I find it hard to believe she's really here in this lonely cemetery."

"She's not here, Arline," Jason countered. "And take it from me, she misses you, too. She's told me several times that leaving her best friend behind was the toughest part of her decision to move on into the next dimension."

Arline's full attention turned on Jason now. "Who are you?" she asked, suddenly suspicious. "I don't remember Sam ever mentioning you."

Jason nervously shifted his weight from one leg to the other. "Well, Arline," he struggled. "I know she mentioned me to you at least once. It was the day the two of you went to the movie together, and later spent the afternoon shopping in the mall. In fact, it was the day you bought that outfit you're wearing right now. By the way, I think you look great in it."

Arline was dumbstruck. "I-I . . . don't understand. How do you know about those things?"

"I was there—for a while at least. Sam got a little perturbed at me and sent me away so she could enjoy the day with you. I didn't actually hear the conversation when she told you about me, but she filled me in later."

Arline gasped, and the color drained from her face. Her legs felt rubbery. "Are you trying to tell me," she choked out, "that you're the one Sam kept referring to as a . . ."

"She used the word 'ghost,' but I prefer being called an angel."

"You're Sam's ghost? But—you don't look like a ghost. Why would she say that?"

Jason grinned. "She had good reason for calling me a ghost, you can be sure."

Arline suddenly felt very uncomfortable. "Well," she began nervously. "It certainly has been a shock meeting you like this. I've wondered hundreds of times what it was Sam was trying to tell me that day." Arline glanced at her watch. "You have no idea how much I'd like to hear the rest of your story, but I'm running very late right now. I barely have time to make it to the station. Here," she said, pulling a business card from her purse and handing it to Jason. "Give me a call at the station. We can talk about it on the air, if you don't mind. I'm sure my listeners will find it fascinating."

Arline watched as the business card slid through Jason's fingers and fell to the ground, but she merely assumed he had accidentally dropped it.

"I'm sorry to rush off like this," she said, hurrying toward her car. "But in my business one can't be late to work. Give me that call, all right?"

CHAPTER TWO

Watching Arline drive away, Jason wondered how she could have seen him. According to Gus, the rules would be the same this time as before. That meant only one person would be allowed to see him, and that was supposed to be Bruce. After all, Bruce was the reason Jason was here. Common sense would make dealing with anyone else unthinkable.

Jason soon learned he wasn't the only one confused by the strange turn of events. Not two minutes after Arline drove away, who should show up but Gus himself. "We have a problem, pal," Gus said, as though he were telling Jason something he didn't already know.

Jason stared at his old friend in disbelief. "It's obvious we have a problem," he said, not trying to hide his irritation. "You're the one who's supposed to control things like this. What happened? Did you make another typo and enter Arline's name where Bruce's should have been?"

"Ya gotta believe me, Jason, I had nothin' ta do with this switch in strategy. I'm just as much in the dark as to what's goin' on as you are. It's evident someone's been meddlin' with my plan, and I gotta say they've left us with a cricket in the ointment for sure."

Jason couldn't help but smile at this. "Fly, Gus," he corrected him. "They've left us with a fly in the ointment."

"Fly, cricket, what's the difference? We still got the problem, and it's a humdinger. Arline Wilson wasn't included in my plan at all. Now that she's seen ya we have no choice but ta deal with it."

"What's the big deal, Gus? She only saw me once. Can't you just put your original plan back into action?"

Gus shook his head. "Can't do that, pal. I'm already in over my head with the higher authorities. If I was ta bend the rules that far, I'd be diggin' a hole for myself I could never crawl out of. And speakin' of the cemetery, what prompted ya ta come here in the first place? All ya had ta do was stick ta the plan, and this would never have happened."

Jason about flipped. "You're the one who left a message on the computer for me to come here. If that was meant to be a joke, how was I supposed to know? I just assumed you'd find a way to lure Bruce here to make contact with me."

"You got a message on the computer? Hey, pal, I didn't put it there. Somethin's rotten in Denver. It's obvious I've got some detective work ta do."

Something in Jason snapped. "I knew it! I knew when I let you talk me into this little game of yours something would go wrong. That's it, Gus, I quit! I'm going home right now!"

"Come on, pal, cut me some slack here. It's not like this is the end of the universe. It's just a little glitch in the plan. I'll snoop out what's goin' on and put a stop to it."

"You'll figure out what's going on?" Jason sighed. "It's a little late for that, wouldn't you say? It's obvious someone doesn't want Bruce married, and they've taken some pretty strong action to prevent it. How am I supposed to get the guy to the altar when I can't even communicate with him? I'm sorry, Gus, but this project has obviously fallen on its face. You know how I hate the idea of deceiving Sam."

Gus interrupted hurriedly. "I give ya my word, Jason. When the time comes ta tell Sam what we've been up to, I'll take the whole blame. She'll understand. But fer now, just let it go with the explanation I fabricated about sendin' ya to a month-long course on celestial chef's training. That'll keep her suspicions satisfied fer the time bein'. And don't forget—this little project is designed ta give her what she wanted from the beginnin'. She's the one that come up with the idea of gettin' Bruce a wife. I tried ta talk her out of it from the first."

Jason's shoulders slumped in defeat. "So help me, Gus, this is the last time I let you talk me into anything. Something goes wrong with everything you touch. And would you mind explaining how I'm supposed to work with Bruce when he can't even see or hear me?"

It was perfectly clear to Gus. "It's obvious, pal," he said. "Ya hafta solicit Arline's help with the project."

Jason snorted. "Oh, sure, just like that. Hi, Arline. You don't know me, but I'm the angel who's married to your best friend, Samantha. I was wondering if you would mind helping me get her old boyfriend married off. It would only mean disrupting your whole life, but that shouldn't be too much to ask."

Gus ignored the sarcasm. "I never said it would be easy, but you can do it, Jase. I've seen ya talk yer way out of tougher fixes than this one. And while yer at it, think about how upset Sam's gonna be if I fail ta hold up my end of the contract in gettin' Bruce a wife. Do ya really want ta face her if that happens?"

"I don't want to do anything to upset Sam," Jason said definitely. "If I do agree to go ahead with this project, I'm telling her about it right up front."

A look of horror suddenly flashed across Gus' face. "No, Jason! Don't even think about such a thing. Let me do this one my way. Much as I love Sam, I don't relish the thought of doin' business with her again. I'll swear that woman could chew up a porcupine."

Jason frowned. "I don't like it, Gus. It doesn't set right with me— hiding things from Sam."

"Don't think of it as hidin' somethin' from her," Gus encouraged him. "Just think of it as puttin' off tellin' her about a few things for a while. Now stop yer arguin' and go catch up with Arline's car before ya lose track of where she's headed."

"But, Gus—"

"Blast it, Jason, time's a wastin'. Go catch up ta that car."

Jason wanted to protest further, but instead he bit his lip and did as Gus had asked. After all, when it came right down to it, he wouldn't be able to face Samantha's disappointment if Bruce's happiness wasn't ensured. After all, she had given up a lot to leave Bruce for Jason. And the thought of hurting Bruce was staggeringly painful for her. With a sigh, Jason slid into the seat next to Arline, who by now was nearly to her office. He folded his arms and smiled over at her.

"What is this?" Arline started at the sight of Jason. "How did you get there?"

"I'll be glad to explain if you'll give me the chance. But it's going to take some understanding on your part, I'm afraid."

Slamming the brake pedal to the floor, Arline brought the car to an abrupt stop at the edge of the street. "I don't know what's going on here!" she nearly shouted. "I'm not accustomed to giving strange men rides in my car. Especially when they sneak in uninvited. Now get out, this instant!"

"I don't want to get you riled, Arline." Jason tried to placate her. "But I have no intention of leaving your car. I give you my word, you have nothing to fear from me. I only want to talk to you."

"I told you to get out! Now do it, or I'll scream so loud the whole city will hear me."

Jason tried to distract her. "I thought you wanted to know more about why Sam called me a ghost. Doesn't it tease your curiosity just a little, wondering how I got in your car while you were doing fifty miles an hour?"

Arline took the bait. "You couldn't have gotten in while I was doing fifty miles an hour. You had to have gotten in back at the cemetery without my seeing you although, for the life of me, I don't know how you did it. What is it you want from me? Why do you insist on hanging around when I've made it plain I want you out of here?"

Jason sighed. "Like I said, all I want is the chance to talk to you. I have no idea how you were able to see me in the first place, but since it happened I'm left with only one option. Like it or not, I need your help with my assignment."

Arline yelled at him again. "I mean it, mister! I'm about to scream if you don't get out of my car!"

"Come on, Arline," he pleaded. "Give me a chance. There's no way I would harm you even if I could. And believe me, as an angel, I couldn't harm you even if I did want to. Angels don't have that ability."

For a long time Arline sat staring at Jason. "All right," she said at length. "You can ride with me to the radio station, but don't ask me to take you anyplace else. I barely have time to make it to work as it is."

Jason sighed with relief. "Fair enough. We can talk while you drive."

Slipping the Toyota into gear, Arline pulled back into the lane of traffic, all the while keeping one eye on Jason. For some reason she couldn't explain, she was certain he was telling the truth about not harming her.

"Do you make frightening women a habit?" she asked. "Or did you single me out as a personal target?"

Jason looked hurt. "That's not fair, Arline. There's nothing I hate worse than frightening people. It's just that I have a very large handicap to overcome in introducing myself to someone for the first time. That's just one more drawback to being an angel among mortals."

"Look," Arline said, "you and I both know there are no such things as angels or ghosts. So why do you keep calling yourself an angel?"

"Oh, no, you're wrong," Jason contradicted her. "I am an angel. And I wish you wouldn't use the word 'ghost' when referring to me. You have no idea how much I hate being called a ghost."

Arline shrugged. "Angel, ghost, what's the difference? One thing for sure, if you're the one Sam was talking about that day at the mall, it's easy to see why she would have called you a ghost. You are pretty convincing."

"That's because I'm telling the truth."

"You're not only convincing, you're persistent, too. The next thing you'll tell me is that your name is Gabriel, right?"

"My name is Jason Hackett."

"Jason Hackett? That has a nice ring to it. You look like someone Sam would have gotten along with. By the way, do you have anything planned for this afternoon?"

Jason looked surprised. "No, not a thing. I did have some plans earlier, but circumstances have changed—thanks to you being able to see me," he said wryly.

Arline gave him a perplexed look. "I have no idea why you keep saying that, but I'd like the chance to learn more about you. How would you like to come to the station with me? We can talk between callers. Who knows, it might add some spice to my program."

"What's this?" Jason said suspiciously. "Not five minutes ago you were ready to scream if I didn't get out of your car, and now you invite me to your studio for an interview?"

Arline laughed. "You just caught me by surprise, that's all. I believe that somehow you knew Sam, and since she was the best friend I've ever known, I want to hear everything you have to tell me about her. Now how about that interview? Are you game?"

"Well," Jason said thoughtfully, "If you want to interview me, I have no objection. But I suggest you do it where the two of us can be alone."

Arline turned to look at him. "Where we can be alone? You're not one of those people who are afraid of a microphone, are you?" The disgust was evident in her tone.

"I'm not afraid of a microphone," Jason said humorously, "but it could prove a little embarrassing to you when no one in your radio audience could hear my voice."

"What?" Arline was confused for a moment by his words.

"You're the only one who can see or hear me, remember?" Jason said pointedly.

"Oh, we're back to that story, are we? Look, anxious as I am to hear all about you, I think it might be better to wait until we get to the studio. Driving the streets of this city is the most dangerous part of my job, and with the traffic today I could do without the distraction this discussion is causing me."

"You might be right. I'd hate to say anything that might cause you to lose your concentration in this traffic. Not as much for my sake," Jason laughed, "as for yours. After all, I have much less to lose."

Arline looked at him and her eyes narrowed slightly, but she let it drop. Ten minutes later she pulled into an assigned parking space behind radio station KSHR.

"Is this where you work?" Jason asked.

"This is the place. Not as glamorous as you may have pictured it, right?"

"Hey, I'm impressed. But about the interview, I really think you should reconsider."

"What is it with people like you, anyway? You carry on a perfectly normal conversation until you get in front of a microphone, then you freeze up like a Minnesota winter. Just think of the mike as a little black ball on a stick. Forget there's anyone out there listening to what you say. You can do it, Jason. Really, there's nothing to it."

Arline stepped out and rounded the car, where she was astounded to find herself face to face with Jason. "You did it again!" she exclaimed in amazement. "How do you keep getting in and out of this car without my even hearing the door?"

"Closed doors don't mean a thing to me, Arline. I'd think by now you would have seen enough proof to know I'm telling the truth about being an angel."

"Yeah, right," she said, pointing to the door leading into the radio station. "Here's a door. Why don't you walk through it?"

"I could walk through it if I wanted to," Jason answered smugly. "But I remember what happened the first time I did that in front of Sam. You have a program to perform. I'd hate to be the cause of you failing to show up."

"Oh, brother," Arline grumbled, opening her own door and stepping inside. "If I didn't want to hear your story so bad, I'd tell you to take a hike." Jason followed her inside before the door had time to close.

"Cutting things a little close there, aren't you, Arline?" Harry, the station engineer, called out as they entered the transmission room. "I thought there for a while I was going to have to dig out the old Elvis albums and do a little double duty here."

Arline merely laughed. "Didn't your mother teach you any patience at all, Harry? I've never been late for a show yet, have I? Where's Fred, anyway? Was he afraid he might have to play a CD or two on my time if I didn't make it by noon?"

"You know Fred. That's exactly what he wanted to avoid. He had me switch to a commercial break and was out the back door faster than Anacin could stop a headache. He was afraid old man Carson would call in and ask him to cover for you, Arline."

"Fred cover for me? Ha, that's a good one. The only thing Fred will ever do for me is get me fired. And the sooner he can do that, the happier he'll be."

"Fred?" Jason asked. "One of your fellow workers?"

Arline looked mildly annoyed. "Yeah, Fred's show runs from eight in the morning until noon. That's when I come in. It's not like Fred hates me personally, he just hates me because I'm female. He thinks a woman has no place in this business and does everything possible to make life miserable for me."

"What's the deal?" Harry spoke with a puzzled tone. "I know that. I've heard you say it a hundred times."

"I wasn't talking to you, Harry. I was explaining to my friend Jason here," Arline explained patiently.

Harry lifted an eyebrow. "Your friend Jason? Say now, there's a cute one even for you, Arline. Does Jason talk back to you as well?"

Arline glared at Harry. She had no way of knowing he could neither see nor hear Jason. Ignoring his remark, she went about the business of setting up her station. After motioning Jason to sit down in the guest chair, she slipped on her headphones and powered up the mike just as the "ON THE AIR" light at the end of the room lit up.

"Good afternoon, all you happy people out there in listeners' world. Arline Wilson here, bringing you all the midmorning talk, music, and news you can stand. We're coming to you from station K-Share, K-S-H-R, where we share the best of everything with you. The best music from the seventies, eighties, and nineties, as well as the best subjects you, our callers, can bring to our telephone lines.

"I'm sure the last four hours with Fred Goodson has lulled many of you out there to sleep, but it's noon now and Arline is here. Get ready for some good times, all you beautiful people. You know the number to call, don't you? WE SHARE or 937-4273. Give us a call with those ideas or requests. My good buddy, Harry the Henchman, is standing by his phone right now. Wouldn't life be great if we all could have jobs like Harry? Nothing to do but wait for the phone to ring."

Harry flipped a thumb off his nose and scrunched his face at Arline, who smiled but didn't let it bother her. "So give us a call to dedicate a memory to that special person in your life. Or better yet, to get the afternoon started with a lively subject of your choosing. And while we're at it, I have a special treat for you today. Actually, I suppose he's more of a special treat for me. But then I deserve a treat now and then, don't you agree?

"I have a studio guest, with whom we'll be talking on and off throughout the show. His name is Jason Hackett. I met Jason less than an hour ago, and I admit bringing him to the show was for purely selfish reasons. Jason tells me that he was acquainted with my dearest friend, Samantha Allen, who died a year ago in a tragic accident. Jason has graciously accepted my hurried invitation to be with us this afternoon. Hopefully he'll tell us how he knew her and perhaps share some fond memories with us. But for now, here we go with three in a row. Put on your warmest smile, and enjoy." Arline switched off her mike as Harry gave her the high sign to indicate that the first CD was on the air.

"What do you think?" she asked Jason. "This isn't so frightening, is it?"

"No, Arline, it's not. And I hope what I have to say won't be too frightening either."

Arline smiled. "You're the strangest man I have ever met, Jason. I hardly know what to expect from you next. If you're worried about frightening me, forget it. You came as close to that as you ever will by showing up unannounced in my car. Now, are you ready to tell me why Sam referred to you as a ghost?"

"Sam loved to call me a ghost because she knew it irked me," Jason spoke earnestly. "In fact she still calls me a ghost every chance she gets. She thinks it's funny."

Arline coughed and placed a hand quickly to her throat. "Let me get this straight," she said, trying to get her voice back to normal. "Sam still talks to you?"

"Yes, Arline. Strange as it sounds, Sam speaks to me all the time. And believe it or not, I even answer her."

"Okay, so I was wrong. You can say something to shock me. One thing for sure, I'm seeing more and more how Sam could have referred to you as a ghost. You're good. It wouldn't surprise me if you really had her convinced you are one."

Jason pulled a face. "Angel, Arline. Call me an angel. I hate being called a ghost."

"All right, let's see if I have this straight," Arline said crisply. "You're a ghost, who doesn't like to be thought of as a ghost. You have a knack for getting in and out of cars so quietly that no one even notices. You hear my best friend Sam talking to you, and you even answer her back. Is that about it?"

"Arline!"

"Okay, okay. You're an angel. Funny, though, you don't look like the kind of angel someone would put on top of a Christmas tree."

"When you find out I'm telling the truth about being an angel, you're going to feel pretty silly, you know that? How about if we cut through some of the preliminaries here? Ask Harry if he sees anyone in here with you, Arline. I think you're in for a real surprise."

Arline didn't look worried. "Yeah, right, ask Harry. I wouldn't put it past Harry if he didn't cook this whole thing up in the first place. He loves to play a good prank on me. Be honest with me, Jason, is Harry at the bottom of this little game?"

"Oh, brother," Jason sighed, standing and walking to the glass that separated the transmission room from Harry's engineering booth. "This is going to be tougher than I thought. I suppose I could walk through this glass, that would remove all doubt. But like I said before, that sort of thing didn't work well when I was proving myself to Sam. She hated me doing that."

"Ha, I was right," Arline laughed. "Harry is pretending not to see you. Well, the two of you aren't fooling me for one second, buster. I intend to play the game out right in front of my audience."

Arline's smile left little doubt that she was pleased with herself for seeing through the practical joke. "I take great pleasure in staying ahead of Harry in the pranks department," she said. "He pulled a good one on me just last week. Right in the middle of my one o'clock news broadcast, he came in here dragging a ten-foot-long rubber snake across my desk. I lost it on the spot. That's when my mike went off until I could quit laughing."

She looked at Jason and said archly, "My audience may never know why they had thirty seconds of silence. I have to admit, Harry got me good with that one. But he isn't about to rattle me with this little angel trick." As if talking to herself, she added musingly, "The one thing I can't figure is how Harry knew I'd be at the cemetery."

Arline ignored Jason as she arranged all her notes carefully. Not until the last bar of the third song, "I Shot The Sheriff," had faded away did she speak. Switching the mike on, she began, "As I promised, it's time to interview our guest, who, by the way, let me in on a big secret while you were enjoying the last three songs. It seems our friend Jason here is an . . . angel. I know what you're thinking out there, but you heard me right. I'm about to interview an angel. Now there's one thing old Fred Goodson has never done. You can bet I'm beating him to the punch on this one. And who knows, I might entice this angel into telling us the true story of what happened to Elvis."

Arline turned to Jason with a huge smile. "Tell me, Angel Jason, how does it feel being interviewed by a mere mortal talk show hostess? And while you're at it, tell us how you've so cleverly hidden your wings beneath that sports shirt you're wearing."

Jason sighed, and shook his head slowly. "You insist on doing this the hard way, don't you, Arline? Okay, I'll play along with your little game. But remember I told you your audience can't hear a word I'm saying. To answer your question about the wings, that's a misconception. Angels don't have wings. For the most part, I look exactly as I did back in the sixties when I was alive. I look a little younger than I did then, but other than that—"

"Did you hear that, audience? Oh, wait. Jason just said you can't hear a word he's saying, didn't he? He's just informed us that angels don't have wings. I don't know about you out there, but this comes as a shock to me. Tell us, Jason, or should I say, tell me so I can pass it on to my listeners? Why is it that angels don't have wings?"

Jason's expression was one of concern. "I hope you don't end up losing your job over this," he said, very seriously.

Arline glanced toward Harry. Just as she had anticipated, he was wearing his best confused look. *Just as I suspected,* she though. *Harry is in on this prank. He's pretending to suppose I'm making a fool out of myself by interviewing someone who really isn't here. Well, it won't work. I refuse to give in to his pressure. I'll play the game out to the end.*

"Just answer the question, Jason, and don't worry about me losing my job. I'm sure everyone out there is holding their breath wondering why angels don't really have wings."

"I'm warning you, Arline. You're just getting in deeper and deeper. I wish you'd listen to me."

"I can't believe this," Arline laughed confidingly to her radio audience. "I have an angel here who doesn't even know anything about being an angel. He tells me angels don't have wings, then can't explain why not. I wish if they were going to send an angel to haunt me, or whatever you call what they do, they would at least send one who knew something about angels."

Jason spoke clearly. "I don't have wings because I'm just a man. I lived my life, and I moved on to the next dimension like everyone has to do when it comes time."

"What a disappointment this is turning into," Arline said into the mike. "My angel is really nothing more than a man. I suppose you're going to tell me next that all angels are nothing more than men, right?"

"Not exactly," Jason laughed. "If Sam were to pay you a visit, I hardly think you'd call her a man. Even a stubborn disc jockey like you couldn't make that mistake."

"Don't call me a disc jockey!" Arline snapped, while holding the mike off. "I hate that term. I'm a talk show hostess, and don't you ever forget it!"

"Aha!" Jason gloated. "You don't like being called a disc jockey. That should give you some idea how I feel being called a ghost."

Arline glared at Jason as if to say, *Let's stick to the subject at hand,* then gave her attention to her audience. "I'd say it's time for a couple more songs, wouldn't you, folks? I've broken the ice on today's show by introducing you to an angel without wings. What do you think out there? Should we take Jason's word for this, or should we pursue the subject further? How can any of us forget the angel Clarence from the old Christmas classic *It's a Wonderful Life?* Wasn't earning his wings the biggest motivation for bringing him here to haunt Jimmy Stewart? What about it? Have any of you out there had an angel experience of your own? Give us a call, and shed some light on this bit of trivia. Do angels have wings, or do they not?"

"I have no idea what you're pulling in there, Arline," Harry said after starting the next CD, "but you have a caller on line one. Would you like to pick it up, or do you want your invisible friend to do it?"

Arline simply smiled and picked up the phone. "Arline Wilson here," she said. "And who do I have on the line this time?"

"My name's Brandy Michaels," came the answer. "I'm a DJ out in Phoenix. I'm here visiting my sister for a week, and happened to hear your exchange with the angel who's really not there. I just wanted to tell you I think it's a great gimmick. If you don't mind, I'd like to use it on my own show sometime."

"Brandy Michaels?" Arline asked suspiciously. "Did you ever work with an engineer named Harry Oliver by any chance?"

"No," Brandy laughed. "Why do you ask?"

"If you're really a DJ then you should understand how nerve-racking these little pranks can be. So help me, if I'm ever in Phoenix I'm going to hunt you out and you know what they say paybacks are, don't you?"

"I'm sorry, Arline, but I have absolutely no idea what you're talking about. I only called to tell you I liked your idea and to ask if you minded me using it."

"You like my idea? Are you trying to make me believe you actually didn't hear Jason answering my questions?"

"Look, I don't know what's going on at your station, but I'd keep an eye on your engineer if I were you. I'm telling you, Jason's voice is not being transmitted. You are the only one I've heard, and I assumed it was a gimmick. A good one, I might add."

Arline looked back to Harry and studied him closely for several seconds before answering Brandy. "I think you're telling me the truth, Brandy," she said, after thinking it over. "I have a hunch Harry's the one pushing the right switches to make me look bad. I'm glad you let me in on this, though. I think I'll just continue to play along with the gag, if it's coming across as good as you say."

"Take it from one who sits in the same chair you do, it's coming across with blue ribbons."

"It's all right with me if you use the idea in Phoenix, Brandy. Thanks to your call, I might just be using it here for a while myself."

With the phone back on the hook, Arline turned to speak to Jason only to discover that he was gone. *How does he do that?* she wondered. *I suppose it doesn't matter. He probably never met Sam anyway. He's probably just some friend of Harry's.*

CHAPTER THREE

Watching Arline at work was fascinating, but Jason soon realized he was making little progress trying to convince her he was an angel. In a way it reminded him of his first meetings with Sam, except Arline had an entire radio audience listening in on her end of the conversation. With this in mind, he decided to put this part of his assignment on hold for the time being. He could always get back to Arline when she was less distracted. For now, he could make better use of his time by checking in on his old friend and rival, Bruce Vincent. *After all, Bruce is the real reason I'm here,* Jason reminded himself.

As luck would have it, finding Bruce proved to be more difficult than he had supposed. Visits of both his home and office came up empty. A visit to Maggie, Gus's secretary, seemed to be in order. Maggie could find Bruce in the time it took to punch in his name on her computer.

Jason paused. *There's always the chance Bruce might be at Jenice Anderson's apartment,* he thought. Unfortunately, Jenice's apartment, too, was empty. Then, just as Jason was about to leave, a picture hanging on the wall caught his attention.

"So that's Jenice," Jason chuckled. "She bears an unbelievable resemblance to her sister, Rebecca Morgan. How well I remember following Bruce and Sam to their dinner at the Morgans. And that awful burned duck for dinner." Jason had not been impressed with Rebecca Morgan's cooking skills. He wondered if Jenice was anything like her sister.

Jason smiled as he remembered the day he first heard the name "Jenice Anderson." He had been sitting alone in Samantha's apartment after she had said good-bye and left to become the wife of

Bruce Vincent. Jason's moment of greatest sorrow had suddenly been transformed into one of indescribable joy when Samantha returned with the promise of never leaving his side again. Reliving the scene as if it had happened only yesterday, he could almost hear Samantha's voice gurgling with excitement.

"I was on my way to marry Bruce when Gus caught me in the elevator. He handed me a new contract, one that would replace the contract altered by his typo. As soon as I read it I knew it was the answer to our problem, but I wanted a few changes in it. Of course, Gus, being the sweetheart he is, didn't argue with me." She gave Gus a big smile.

"What can I say, Sam? It's just my big streak of generosity!"

"Sure, Gus. Your generosity, plus the fact you knew it was the only way I'd sign the new contract."

"That might have had something to do with it," he shrugged.

"I learned a long time ago, if you want something, go after it with everything you have. The thing I wanted most was a certain ghost who's been haunting me for the last few months. But I figured Gus owed us something a little extra, for the trouble his typo put us both through.

"What did you get out of him, Sam?" Jason asked.

"I think I did well, you know, for a schoolteacher, I mean." She grinned. *"I added several things to his proposed contract, including the 'Bruce clause.'*

"The 'Bruce clause'? I'm probably going to be sorry for asking, but what is the 'Bruce clause'?"

I just couldn't bear to hurt Bruce," she sighed. *"So I negotiated a wife for him."*

"You did what?"

"Maggie ran it through the computer, and it came up with the perfect match for him. Her name is Jenice Anderson. Jenice is Rebecca Morgan's sister. You remember Rebecca, don't you?"

"The burnt duck?"

"That's her," Samantha chuckled. *"Gus had to guarantee they would be married within a year. But wait until you hear the best part. Gus has a way figured out for Bruce to meet Jenice—at my funeral."*

"Oh, brother! That sounds like something Gus would come up with. Although it is sort of fitting, at that."

"How so?" she asked.

"Knowing Bruce, I figure if he meets his wife at a funeral, it may be the most interesting date they'll ever have."

"Jason Hackett! You're still jealous of Bruce, aren't you?"

"I do have feelings, you know. How do you think I felt watching you kiss him? And that constant 'darling' thing drove me nuts."

"What are you fretting about? You got me in the end, didn't you? And, I have to admit, you're a lot cuter than him, even if you are a ghost."

"I'm not a ghost, and anyway he's a wimp. How do you know Jenice will go for the guy?"

Gus had snorted. *"Compared to you and Sam, this one's a piece of cake. Consider it history."*

Jason's thoughts returned to the present. "A piece of cake?" he grumbled to himself. "Sure, Gus. You guaranteed Bruce and Jenice would be married within a year. Now with more than half that time gone, I'm back on earth playing angel again—this time on the premise of fanning the blaze between Bruce and Jenice. I sure wish Gus would learn to manage his affairs better so Sam and I could get on with our lives together."

Jason's thoughts were interrupted by the sound of Jenice's phone ringing. After the third ring, the caller gave up, but not before Jason's attention was drawn to a note pad next to the phone. He read, "Bruce, 11:30, The Hunter's Cottage."

"Well, what do you know?" Jason smiled. "A bit of good luck for a change. They must be having lunch there now."

* * *

Sure enough, Bruce and Jenice were there, seated at a table on the lakeside patio. In a way it was like old times, spying on one of Bruce's dates. Except when Samantha was involved, it was more personal.

"But darling," Bruce said, holding one of Jenice's hands across the table, "you promised to marry me next month. We already have all the arrangements made for the wedding. Why are you having second thoughts now?"

Boy, does that sound familiar or what? Jason rolled his eyes. *It could be a recording of the way he pressured Sam to go to the altar with him.*

I'm not sure I can handle this assignment. It brings back too many memories of the wimp. Already I want to throw up.

"It's not that I don't care for you, Bruce," Jenice explained. "Because I do. The problem is in our life styles. You have to agree, the two of us have almost nothing in common. After giving more consideration to what spending a lifetime together would be like, I'm not as sure as I thought I was."

"That's preposterous, Jenice. I know I can make you happy, if you'll only give me the chance. I realize it's been hard on you, with the trouble I've had forgetting Samantha and all. But I give you my word, I'll never let her memory stand in the way of my feelings for you."

"I'm sure you mean to make me happy, and I understand your feelings for Samantha. Losing her to such a tragic accident, on your wedding day of all things, was a terrible blow. But I could live with that. What I'm afraid I can't live with is the obvious gap in our personalities. I just want certain things out of life, and I'm having a very difficult time convincing myself to give up all my dreams, regardless how foolish those dreams may seem to you."

Bruce sighed. "Oh, darling, what could possibly be so important about climbing the highest mountain in the world? Don't you realize that only a few hundred people have ever reached the top of Mount Everest? And they were the most qualified mountain climbers in the world. Why can't you settle for a nice peaceful hike through the canyons behind my parents' home in the mountains? You have to admit that's a much more sensible thing to do."

Jenice shook her head. "More sensible, yes. But nowhere near as satisfying. Edmund Hillary and his partner Tenzing Norgay were the first to ever reach the summit of Mount Everest, and they did it on May 29, 1953. That was the day my mother was born. She always dreamed of following in the footsteps of those two great mountaineers, but she settled instead for marriage to my father. She loves my father and they've been happy, but she had to sacrifice her dreams to be his wife. Over the years, when I was a little girl, she passed those dreams on to me. Now I see myself facing the same choice my mother did when my father asked her to marry him. Do you understand what it is I'm trying to say?"

"I—I think so, darling, but—"

"I know you find this hard to comprehend, Bruce, but it's not as important to actually reach the summit of Mount Everest as it is to try. And climbing mountains is not the only dream my mother instilled in me. There are countless other exciting things I want to do in my lifetime. I want to go on an African safari someday. In fact, if anything, I want to go on safari even more than I want to attempt Mount Everest. I want to explore the inside of a volcano, and pilot a fighter jet, and do many more exciting things with my life. I'm sorry, Bruce. We both know those kinds of things are just not *you.*"

Bruce gulped. "Perhaps, darling, I could learn to enjoy some of those things. If you'll give me a little time."

Ha! Jason laughed. *A wimp like you climb a mountain or go on a safari? I hardly think so, Bruce. I think I owe Jenice an apology. I was judging her by her sister, and I can see it was a mistake. Rebecca must have taken after her father's side of the family. I'll tell you one thing, Jenice is more woman than you deserve. I wonder how Maggie's computer ever came up with her name as a likely partner for you? You don't suppose . . . Is it possible the computer sees a quality buried somewhere deep in your soul that the rest of us have overlooked? Now there's a staggering thought. If it's true, that quality must be buried as deep as Mount Everest is high.*

"The biggest problem, Bruce," Jenice went on to say, "is that I can't bring myself to believe you're the kind of man who could ever change that much. My father never did. And it's not that I don't love my father, it's just that I wish he could have been more adventuresome. For my mother's sake, that is."

Bruce's voice became almost pleading. "I can change, Jenice. I'm a psychologist. I help people change all the time. If I can help them, what's to keep me from helping myself?"

"I don't know," Jenice replied skeptically. "I have a hard time picturing you on the Matterhorn at Disneyland, let alone doing the kinds of things I long to do."

"I agree it would be difficult for me," Bruce contended. "But don't I at least deserve the chance to try?"

"All right," Jenice agreed, with a deep sigh. "I'll make a deal with you. If you want to marry me enough to change your lifestyle, I'll give you the chance. I'm not going to make it easy on you, though."

Bruce removed a handkerchief from his inside coat pocket and wiped his forehead. "What exactly do you have in mind, darling?" he asked nervously.

Jenice was silent for what seemed a very long time. At last she spoke, at the same time removing Bruce's ring from her finger.

"I'm going to put our engagement on hold for now," she said, pushing the ring into his hand. "If you can prove to me you're willing and capable of changing into a man who loves a challenge the way I do, I'll proceed with our marriage as planned. Otherwise—"

"I can do it, darling," Bruce quickly interjected. "I can make all the changes you want. You'll just have to give me some time, that's all."

Jenice shook her head violently. "Oh, no you don't, Bruce. I'm not buying one of your stall tactics. I know you well enough to realize where a 'later on' promise will end up with you. The prospect of spending our lives together is much too important to be taken lightly."

"Very well, darling," Bruce conceded painfully. "What is it you want me to do?"

"Let me think on it a little while," she answered. "I want to be fair, but I want to present you with a challenge hard enough to prove you not only have the desire to change, but the ability as well."

Interrupted by the appearance of the waiter at their table, Bruce said no more for the moment. Jason watched as they were being served. *The lobster doesn't look too bad,* he thought. *Not as good as mine, of course. But not bad, nevertheless.*

For several minutes the two of them ate quietly. It was Jenice who first broke the silence. "I've come up with an idea that I find acceptable, Bruce. I'm not sure you're going to like it, though."

Bruce lowered his fork and wiped the corner of his mouth with the napkin he was holding. As he spoke, his words came with great difficulty.

"You're probably right, darling. I'm sure I won't like any idea that forces me to prove my ability to change. Believe it or not, I do know how difficult it is for a woman who loves life the way you do to be satisfied with a boring man like me. Samantha was a great deal like you, Jenice. Not that she particularly wanted to go on an African safari or climb the world's highest mountain, but she did have a passionate love for life—like you. Strange as it may seem, you and Samantha are the only two women I have ever been the least bit interested in. Perhaps there's a reason for my attraction to adventure-loving women. I don't know. This much I do know, however. When I lost Samantha, my life would have been in ruin if it hadn't been for you stepping in to fill the void. Now I face the prospect of losing you." There was a long pause before Bruce added, "Tell me your plan, darling. I must know what it is you require of me."

Jenice looked down. "You're certainly not making this easy for me, Bruce. I hope you know how much I admire you. The last thing I want to do is hurt you, but . . ."

"I understand, Jenice," Bruce said gently. "Just tell me what it is you want me to do."

Jenice looked up and gazed steadily at Bruce. "Well, if you really want to prove your ability to change, the challenge I have in mind will give you the chance. I'm offering you a month to prepare for the challenge. That should give you sufficient time. For that month, we won't see or contact each other at all. No dates, no telephone calls, no contact at all. Then one month from today, on April the fifteenth, we'll put your challenge to the test. At exactly noon on that day, I'll wait for you on the stretch of private beach belonging to your friend Howard Placard. If you meet the challenge at that time, I'll put your ring back on my finger. On the other hand, if you don't meet the challenge, it can only mean the two of us would never be happy together."

She took Bruce's hand gently in her own. "Now for the clincher. When you show up on the beach, it must be by parachuting from the sky. Do you think you can do that?"

Bruce turned three shades of green as he thought about what Jenice was asking of him. "A parachute?" he echoed feebly. "You mean—you want me to jump from an airplane?"

Jenice nodded. "That's the general idea, Bruce. I figure if you can accomplish that feat in one month, it will prove you have what it takes to become the kind of man I want to spend my life with."

"Oh, boy," Jason said, feeling a little ill himself. "This is going to be a lot tougher assignment than I had supposed. You may be in big trouble, Gus."

CHAPTER FOUR

The red numbers on the clock next to Arline's bed had passed the two-thirty mark before thoughts of Jason Hackett faded, allowing Arline to fall into an exhausted sleep. Who could this man be? Why had he suddenly shown up in her life, claiming to be an angel? How could he be so brazen as to claim he actually talks to Samantha? He had to be one of Harry's cronies recruited to help with the master prank of all time. *But still—what if . . . ?* She pushed the thought away. *That would be impossible. There's no such things as angels, or ghosts, or whatever you call them.*

When sleep at last came, it was only to take her mind through that fascinating door into another world where dreams bring to life moments long lost to reality. That night, she was with Samantha again. It was wonderful to be with her friend again. Not only did Arline relive many of the special moments the two had shared growing up together, she also met and conversed with the Samantha Jason had described to her. Never had a dream seemed so real. Never had she wanted a dream to be real as much as this one.

Brrriiinnngg!

Why does the phone always interrupt the best dreams? Arline grumbled.

"Stewart Carson, here," came the curt response. "Sorry to call so early, Arline. But I'm on my way to a day full of meetings, and we need to talk."

Stewart Carson was a man of many enterprises, including the ownership of station KSHR, where Arline worked. A call at home from Stewart usually meant Arline was in trouble, and being in trouble with that man was never pleasant.

"Yes, sir, Mr. Carson," she managed, the muscles of her body cringing with apprehension.

"I heard your little 'angel' gimmick on yesterday's show."

Suddenly, Arline was wide awake. "The 'angel' gimmick? Yes, sir, I can explain that. You see, Harry—"

"It's all right, Arline. Right now I don't have time to listen to how you came up with the gimmick. Just let me say I had intended to use this call for the purpose of firing you, but I can hardly do that in light of what's happened. It seems the station has been flooded with calls about your angel. All of them positive. Your audience loved the gimmick, though for the life of me I can't understand why. Calls like that can mean only one thing; our ratings are up. I like it when our ratings go up, and I'm one who likes to show my gratitude when someone finds a way to make that happen. Now, listen carefully to what I'm about to tell you. I only have time to say this once."

He liked the "angel" thing? Arline mulled, sitting upright in bed. *Boy, have you outsmarted yourself this time, Harry.* The smile on her lips grew even wider as she listened to Stewart's reason for the call.

"For several weeks now I've been toying with the idea of starting an afternoon talk show at my television station. Last Wednesday I approached my advisers with the idea and they liked it. They liked it so much, they gave me the green light to put together a format for the show. I was planning to offer the job to Fred Goodson, but after your ingenuity with the angel gimmick I'm having second thoughts. Your gimmick could be just what the show needs to set it apart from all the other talk shows out there on the networks. Would you be interested in a shot at the job, Arline? I'm not saying anything's definite, you understand."

"A chance to have my own talk show on television?!" she shouted excitedly into the phone. "Yes! I'd give up a year's worth of chocolate for a chance at the position. Please, Mr. Carson, tell me what you want me to do."

"I'll have to fill you in on the details later, but I'm planning a little contest, so to speak, between you and Fred. I'd like to see how each of you handle yourselves under pressure. I still have to work out the finer points, but basically I'll have you and Fred in front of a panel of professionals. The panel will shoot questions at the two of you to test your knowledge of certain subjects and your ability to remain poised under fire. I talked to Fred yesterday, and you might as well know he's a little bent out of shape about my considering you for the position. He has the idea there are already too many women doing talk shows. I just want you to know I don't agree with him on that point, and after a little man-to-man talk he understands that now. I let him know that as the boss I have the right to do what ever I darn well please about filling new positions. Bottom line is, Fred agrees to the contest. How about you, Arline? Can I count you in?"

"Yes, sir," she quickly agreed, not even trying to hide the excitement in her voice.

"Fine, then. I'll be getting back to you with the particulars after I do some fine-tuning on the idea. Keep up with your new gimmick on today's show. I'll be listening, and so will your audience. Keep us all happy, Arline. Especially me."

Arline's intended reply never made it past her throat. The sound of Stewart abruptly hanging up made the reply unnecessary.

"Yes!" she shouted to herself, still clutching the phone tightly as she thrust both hands high over her head. "The fourth of July will be a national holiday in London before old Fred can out-think me in any contest Stewart comes up with."

Singing in the shower wasn't something Arline made a habit of, but on this particular morning she not only went through three musicals, but threw in a couple of old Beatles albums for good measure. *And to think Daddy tried to talk me into being an interior decorator. He'll have to admit he was wrong now. I'm going to host the greatest talk show of all time. I can see it in my mind now. Good evening, ladies and gentlemen. This is Arline Wilson bringing you the chance to vent your ideas on the hottest subjects of the hour. Whether it's the latest from around the corner, or around the world, this is the place you'll hear it dissected best.*

Today's subject—Fred Goodson, former amateur disc jockey for a local radio station, was seen peddling pencils from a cup in front of our studio earlier this afternoon. He's being held without bail on suspicion of robbing the blind to get the pencils. You may remember Fred from the days when I was livening up the airways with my witty show on station KSHR. Fred was the little-known upstart that put the microphone to sleep just ahead of my show every morning. You might have caught a

word or two from him if you ever turned your radio on a couple of min-
utes early to catch my show.

Now it's time for you, the audience, both at the studio and in your
homes, to tell us how you feel about Fred being deported to the North
Pole. Is the judge being too tough on this criminal, or is he getting exactly
what he deserves? Let's hear those phone lines jingle as I talk with my first
guest here at the studio. And don't forget, I'll have the expert opinion
from my friend Jason the angel at the end of the show.

Arline was just sitting down to a breakfast of milk, half a grape-fruit and, a slice of toast when she happened to glance over the top of the newspaper she had been engrossed in. There, leaning nonchalantly against her refrigerator with his arms folded and legs crossed, was Jason Hackett.

"What are you doing in my house?!" she screamed, dropping the paper and knocking over her chair while leaping to her feet.

"I told you, Arline, I'm an angel. Angels go wherever we want, and we never knock."

"You're good," Arline said, regaining her composure and glaring at him. "I'll give you that. You're not only sneaky, but you must be a locksmith, too. I know you don't have a key to my place. But you can go back and tell your friend Harry that his little joke backfired, my friend."

"You're referring to Stewart Carson's proposal, I assume?"

Caught off guard by this remark, Arline sank slowly to the chair she had just returned to the upright position. "You know about Stewart's offer? But how?"

"I heard your conversation with him on the phone."

"You were in my bedroom?!"

"Oh, no," Jason responded quickly, holding out his hands in a defensive gesture. "Sam cured me of that long ago. I was in the adjoining room."

"You're a liar! You couldn't possible have heard my conversation with Stewart from there."

"Yes, I could," Jason smiled. "Angels not only go where they want, they have good hearing, too. You might as well give up the struggle. You're going to have to admit I'm an angel sooner or later, and it will save us both a lot of trouble if it's sooner. Then we can get on with the more serous business at hand."

"Forget it, buster! You and I have nothing more to discuss. You can just let yourself out the same door you came in. And do it now!"

"Can't do that, Arline. It's not my fault you happened to be the one chosen to see and hear me, but you were. So it leaves me in need of your help, and I'm not going away until you give it to me."

"This has ceased to be funny, Jason Hackett. I have no idea how you learned about Stewart's offer, but you were either in my bedroom or—" She stopped in midsentence as a frightening thought came to her. "Or Stewart is in on the prank himself. Oh, no—that must be it. He's not really offering me the chance to be a talk show hostess at all. It's all part of Harry's cruel joke. I hate you, Jason. You can tell Harry I hate him, too. I'd better not hate Mr. Carson, though. I still need this job."

Jason drew in a deep breath and walked up to where Arline was still seated at the table. "I can see why you're Sam's best friend," he snickered. "When it comes to jumping to wrong conclusions, you're exactly like her. I didn't want to have to do it this way, but you leave me little choice. Here," he said, extending his hand toward her, "shake my hand."

Arline glared even harder at him. "No!" she barked. "Why should I shake your hand when you're in cahoots with the enemy?"

"Arline!" Jason retorted in a voice so filled with authority it caught her completely off guard. "Shake my hand!"

Arline's chin dropped an inch, and her eyes grew three sizes at the sound of his voice. Slowly, she extended her hand toward his. Instead of the expected feeling of warm skin, she felt absolutely nothing as her hand passed completely through his. "What is this?!" she screamed, pulling her hand quickly back. "Your hand was right in front of me." She tried to calm herself. "I know, Harry has come up with a way to make you appear as a hologram."

"A hologram?" Jason protested in disgust. "That's almost as bad as being called a ghost. What's the matter with you? Why is it so hard to accept the fact that I'm an angel? What more can I do to prove it to you?"

"Please," Arline pleaded. "Tell me Stewart's offer is real. Whatever else you may do to me with this elaborate joke, I can handle. But that offer has to be real. It's the dream of a lifetime."

"I give you my word, the offer is real. And what's more, I'll do anything I can to help you get the position. I say that not only because I honestly want to help you, but also because I need your help with a problem of my own."

"I want to believe you, Jason. I want to believe everything you've told me." Arline was thinking of her dream, and of how wonderful it was to think Samantha was alive and well in another dimension. With all her heart, she wished it could be true. But—believing Jason was actually an angel was just a little too far-fetched.

"All right," Jason relented. "We'll let it go with your accepting me as a hologram for now. At least that will explain why I can't open doors for you and the like."

Arline rose to her feet and slowly extended a hand toward the side of Jason's face. He made no effort to avoid her attempt. Once again she felt nothing.

"I don't understand this hologram thing, either," she admitted. "But I know they're doing some amazing things with technology these days. Which brings up a question. Why is Harry so obsessed with his prank to go to this much trouble and expense?"

"I know you have a hard time understanding this, Arline. But Harry has nothing to do with why I'm here. I'll tell you who does have a lot to do with it, though, and that's your best friend and my wife, Sam."

Arline gaped at him. "Your *wife?* Now that's carrying this joke a little far, wouldn't you say? As much as it pains me to say it, Sam's dead. She can't be anyone's wife. And if she was still alive, she'd be Bruce Vincent's wife. She was killed on the day the two of them were to be married."

"You know what your problem is, Arline? Your problem is, you don't know any more about dying than you know about angels. It's true, Sam's not in her body just now, but she is alive. Not only is she alive, she's still the same old Sam you knew and loved when she was here with you. The reason she's married to me instead of Bruce is a long story. I'll be glad to tell it to you sometime, but for now there are more pressing matters we need to discuss."

For a long time, Arline stood with her eyes fixed on Jason. Slowly she circled him, looking at him carefully from every angle. Having made the full circle, she faced him once more.

"I'd give anything to believe you really are an angel, and that Sam is as alive and happy as you claim she is. Just on the off-chance that is what you really are, what is this pressing business you keep bringing up?"

"The problem," Jason answered, obviously relieved that Arline was ready to listen to him, "is Bruce Vincent."

"Bruce Vincent? I don't understand. What possible interest could you have in Bruce?"

"Let me answer your question with a question of my own, Arline. What if Sam had asked you to make certain Bruce found someone else after she was taken from him? What would you do?"

"That is a ridiculous question. Sam didn't ask anything like that of me."

"Please, Arline," Jason begged. "I'm trying to make a point here. Just for the sake of argument, let's assume Sam had asked you to help Bruce. What would you do about it?"

Arline pursed her lips thoughtfully. "Sam was my best friend. I loved her like the sister I never had, Jason. I would have done anything she ever asked of me."

"Even to the point of helping Bruce find a wife?"

Arline was growing impatient. "Yes, even to that point. But like I said—"

Jason held up his hands. "Let me finish before you completely shut that door, okay? I want you to think back to the day when you last saw Sam. She kept trying to tell you something that you didn't understand, do you remember?"

"How could I ever forget?" Arline laughed. "She told me she was being haunted by a ghost. 'Is his name Casper, by any chance?' I said. Then, just as serious as I've ever seen her, she told me his name was . . ." Arline went suddenly white, and her knees nearly buckled under her as she stared at this strange man. "She told me his name was Jason, and that he was in love with her."

"Now we're getting somewhere," Jason broke in. "Go on, what else took place in your conversation that day?"

"I—I feel a little faint," Arline said. "Could we go to the living room, where I can sit down?"

"What about your breakfast?"

"Somehow I don't think I can face that grapefruit just now," she said, moving toward the living room where she fell limply to the sofa.

Jason followed, but remained standing. "What else did you and Sam say to each other that day?" he pressed. Arline closed her eyes and slowly it came back to her. She had just finished paying for the green pants suit bought at Casual Corners.

"How about a frozen yogurt?" Arline had said as she and Samantha left Casual Corners. "I'll treat."

Samantha was quick to accept. "Make it chocolate, and you've got a deal."

They passed several stores on their way to the food court. Finally Arline spoke up. "You're acting peculiar today, Sam. Why not open up and tell Dr. Arline what's going on?"

Samantha gave a rueful smile. "You can always see right through me. I do have a problem, and it's one I could use some advice with."

"So, let's have it."

"I'm being haunted by a ghost."

Arline's laugh was loud enough to attract the attention of everyone around. "Now that's not your everyday problem. Is his name Casper, by any chance?"

"No," Samantha had said slowly. "His name is Jason, and he's in love with me."

When Arline had accused her of eating too much Red Baron Pizza, Samantha had defended herself. "Oh, no," she said. "My ghost is real. He's very handsome, and he's a real gentleman."

Playing along with her friend, Arline had asked if Sam was in love with her ghost. Sam didn't answer right away. "I'm not sure," she said at last.

Arline studied her carefully, but made no immediate reply. They reached the frozen yogurt counter, where she ordered two large chocolate cones. Only after they had taken a seat at a nearby table did she speak again. "Does Bruce know about this ghost?"

Samantha took a deep breath. "Yes," she answered. "Bruce knows about him."

"Well, what does he think about it all?"

"Bruce dislikes him, immensely."

"Samantha," Arline said, looking Samantha in the eye, "Jason is no ghost, is he? There's another man in your life, isn't there? Are you involved with a married man?"

Samantha looked at her aghast. "Now why would you think a thing like that, Arline?"

"You are still planning to marry Bruce, aren't you?" Arline asked her.

At this, Sam had backed off and changed the subject. "I'm a little confused about things, right now. Enough about me. Eat your yogurt."

But Arline wasn't going to let her off the hook so easily. "I've never been able to understand what it is you see in Bruce, but you are wearing his ring. That should mean you owe him something, shouldn't it?"

"I'm sure I'll end up married to Bruce," Samantha said firmly. "I've just had some other things to think about."

"You mean the ghost?" Arline said wryly. She was surprised to see tears in Samantha's eyes.

"Are you going to tell me the truth about your 'ghost' boyfriend?" Arline asked.

"He is a ghost," Sam said stubbornly. "You can believe me or not, as you choose. If you don't like the idea of him being a ghost, then make up something else. He is real, he does love me, and he has me very confused."

Arline sighed. "What kind of a best friend would I be if I didn't trust you? We'll call him a ghost, okay? Now, do you want to talk about him?"

"Yes, Arline," Sam answered, the tears now flowing freely. "I would like to talk about him. He's the best thing that ever happened to me. I have so much fun just being around him."

"I'll ask you again. Do you love him?"

"I'm not sure. I feel completely different about him than I feel about Bruce, that's all I can say."

"Why not just give Bruce his ring back, and stick with this—ghost?"

"It's not that simple, Arline. Unless a miracle should happen, Jason and I could never have a normal life together."

Arline handed Samantha a napkin, as her untouched yogurt was beginning to drip on the table. "If you didn't want that thing, why didn't you say so before I bought it?"

"I'm sorry," Samantha said, wiping up the spill and taking a big bite. "Let's change the subject. I know how hard it is for you to part with your money."

"Well," Arline said reluctantly, "just remember I'm always here if you need to talk. You know I won't think less of you, no matter what."

"I know, Arline, and thanks. Just talking to you this much has helped a bunch. Now hurry up and get that yogurt down. We still have to find something for me to buy."

Arline looked at Jason and frowned. She had tried to forget that strange conversation with her friend. It was a part of the whole nightmare of losing her best friend, something she didn't like to remember.

"I'm telling you the truth, Arline," Jason said, breaking into her thoughts. "I am the 'ghost' Sam told you about, although I prefer being called an angel. The whole story is long and detailed, but in a nutshell, Sam and I were in love. I have a friend, Gus Winkelbury, who's in charge of certain special conditions pertaining to the dimension where Sam and I live now. Sam negotiated a contract with Gus that allowed the two of us to be together, as we both wanted. One thing in Sam's contract, however, was the stipulation that Bruce be assured of finding someone he could be happy with. It was a requirement that he be married within a year from the day the contract was signed."

Arline closed her eyes and put her hands to her head. "Hold on a minute, Jason. I need you to slow down a bit. I'm a little overwhelmed at the moment. I mean, your story sounds good and all, but I can't quite bring myself to believe you're an angel. How do I know you didn't somehow overhear my conversation with Sam and concoct this whole crazy scenario?"

"Come on, Arline! What else can I do?" Jason looked desperate. "You tell me how I can prove myself to your satisfaction."

Arline thought about it as she watched Jason pace nervously back and forth in front of the sofa. "What did we have to eat at the mall that day?" she asked.

Jason threw his hand up in the air. "I don't know," he said. "I wasn't actually there when the two of you were talking. Sam told me about the conversation later. I'll tell you what I can do, though. I can ask her and give you an answer, say sometime tomorrow. Will that help?"

"It might," Arline replied. "But I can tell you something that will help a lot more. There was a pet name I used to call Sam. I never said the name in front of anyone else, because she hated it. I only called her by the name when I wanted to get her riled. If you can talk to Sam, like you claim, ask her to tell you the name. If you can do that, then I'll believe you."

"But if she hated the name, why would she tell it to me?"

"That should be no problem. Just explain to her why you need to know."

"I can't do that, Arline. I've been sworn to secrecy on my assignment down here. In fact, Sam is the last person Gus will allow me to tell about it."

"I see," Arline said with a cynical smile. "You're just finding excuses why you can't come up with the name. I was right about you in the first place, wasn't I? You are part of Harry's prank after all, aren't you?"

The look of disgust on Jason's face told exactly how he was feeling inside. "No, Arline," he answered insistently. "I'm not part of Harry's prank, and I'm not here to cause problems of any kind for you. I am an angel, and I'm here because some sort of mix-up brought our lives together and now I need your help. If learning your pet name for Sam is the only way I can convince you my story is real, then I'll just have to find a way to pry it out of her."

Taken aback by the forcefulness in Jason's voice, Arline could only watch as Jason walked to the front door.

"I'm leaving for now," he said, pausing at the door and looking back at her. "But you can bet I'll be back just as soon as I can learn the name from Sam." Then, while she watched in total amazement, he simply stepped through the closed door and was gone.

CHAPTER FIVE

Thoughts of Jason Hackett returned with haunting frequency over the next few days. Try as she might, Arline couldn't shake him from her mind. Was it possible he really was an angel, as he claimed? Or, was he something else? She could still be right about him being part of a prank Harry was planning. Or he might be nothing more than a figment of her imagination. Doubts grew stronger as the days stretched into a week, and still he had not returned.

One thing that was real, however, was the gigantic boost Jason Hackett had brought to her radio talk show. The angel gimmick really worked; her audience loved it. Ratings increased overnight, and by the end of the first week seven new commercial contracts had been secured. Stewart Carson was ecstatic and had soon shifted his efforts for creating a television talk show into high gear. Still, Stewart insisted that Arline perform in front of the panel before he offered the new show to either Arline or Fred. By the week's end, Stewart had all the details worked out. The contest was set for Friday afternoon immediately following her radio show. It was to be held in the conference room adjoining Stewart's private office.

Getting through Friday's broadcast proved tougher for Arline than anything else she had ever done. The hands on the transmission room clock moved so slowly she wondered if they were glued to the face. At last, however, time did pass. The excitement was almost more than she could bear as she took her seat in front of the two women and four men who made up the panel. Her eyes shifted to Fred, who was already sitting in his place when she arrived. She was glad to see he looked nervous as he fiddled with his glasses. Her already high state of confidence was boosted even further by his case of nerves. There was little doubt she could outperform him with ease.

It was then that she heard the unexpected voice.

"Hi, Arline. Did you miss me?"

A quick glance over her left shoulder confirmed her greatest fear. There, wearing a very bright grin, stood Jason Hackett. Whether he was an angel or a trick of her imagination, there he stood in all his glory. Of all the times for him to make a reappearance, this was the worst he could have picked. At the moment, she needed to commit all her effort and concentration to the contest. Now she had to deal with Jason Hackett as well. It just wasn't fair.

"What are you doing here now?" she mumbled to him between clenched teeth, hoping no one else would hear. "Can't you see I'm a little tied up at the moment?"

Jason lifted an eyebrow. "You should be grateful I chose this time to check up on you, Arline. You have a problem. Your friend Fred Goodson has the contest rigged in his favor."

"What?" Arline gasped, forcing herself not to be obvious. "What do you mean he has the contest rigged?"

"Just what I said. Fred has a concealed microphone in his tie, and a miniature earphone hidden in the frame of his glasses. His cousin, Andrew Doyle, is in the next room with a computer."

"Are you trying to tell me—?" Arline was flabbergasted.

"I'm telling you Fred is set up to use a computer for finding the answer to any question the panel comes up with." The serious expression on Jason's face told Arline that he was telling her the truth.

Anger sparked from Arline's eyes as her face turned several shades of red. It was all she could do to hold her voice at a level only Jason could hear. "I don't believe it! This is a low point even for Fred Goodson. If you're sure this is true, I'll tell Stewart about this little scheme."

Jason frowned. "I don't think that's a good idea, Arline. Fred would just cover everything up and deny the charges. You'd only end up looking like a fool."

"But—I can't possibly compete against a computer."

"Yes you can." Jason grinned at her. "You have an angel on your side. A darn good one, I might add. I've had experience at this sort of thing before. Just sit tight, and do your best to answer the first question or two. I have to pay a visit to an old friend, then I'll be back with the cavalry. I give you my word, Fred's scheme doesn't hold a chance against what I have in mind."

"Please," Arline begged, "don't play games with me about something this important. My whole future is riding on this contest. I still think I'd be ahead to expose these culprits right up front."

Jason shook his head firmly. "No, Arline. Trust me on this one. I know what I'm doing."

"All right," she agreed reluctantly. "I'll trust you. But if you let me down . . ."

"I won't let you down. Now do as I say, and I'll be back in less time than it takes for one of your commercial breaks."

Arline looked on in amazement as Jason turned and passed through the closed door with ease, just as he had done the last time she watched him leave her house. *Maybe he really is an angel,* she thought. *For your sake, Arline Wilson—you had better hope he is.*

At that moment, Arline's attention was drawn to Stewart Carson, who had just risen to address the group. "As you know," he began, "I've assembled this contest to determine which of these two will become the host or hostess," he added politely, looking at Arline, "of my new television show. I've composed a list of pertinent questions to be asked alternately to each contestant. When a question is directed to Arline, she'll be given the first opportunity to answer it. If she fails to answer correctly, then Fred will have his chance at her question. It works the other way when the question is directed to Fred. The two of you are being judged not only for your knowledge, but also for your charisma in front of the panel. Are there any questions before we begin?"

"I have no questions," Fred answered confidently. "Let's just get on with it."

Arline glared at Fred and toyed with the idea of exposing him right now. She knew, however, that Jason was right. Fred would only make her look ridiculous by pretending innocence. With a sigh, she answered, "I have no questions, either, Mr. Carson."

"Very well," Stewart responded. "Let's get on with it. The first question is yours, Arline. Good luck."

As Stewart took his seat, one member of the panel, an older gentleman with a face resembling a bulldog, pulled a set of cards from his briefcase. Arline knew little about this man other than that he was a longtime consultant to Stewart, and his name was Nelson Oversby. After sliding on a pair of glasses, Nelson read the first question in a voice that matched his face perfectly.

"'The liberation of Kuwait has begun,'" he said, then paused to look up at Arline for effect. "With this announcement," he continued, "the White House Press Secretary broke the news to the American public that war against Iraq had been launched by armed forces of the United Nations. Your question, young lady, is this. Who was the White House Press Secretary at the time?"

"Marlin Fitzwater," Arline answered without hesitation.

"Very good," Nelson replied gruffly. Then, turning to Fred, he stated, "Now it's your turn, young man. Can you tell us the date this event occurred?"

Fred fumbled with a pencil he was holding and appeared deep in thought. It was obvious to Arline what he was doing. He was giving his cousin Andrew time to look up the answer on the computer. Sure enough, after a few seconds, Fred answered. "I believe that declaration was made on January 16, 1991."

"That's exactly right," Nelson said. "So far it would seem that both of you are well versed in your political knowledge."

"May I add something to my answer?" Fred asked smugly.

"Certainly," Nelson answered. "You may expand on your answer if you wish."

"I'd just like to add that the war began at approximately 6:40 in the evening on the day mentioned. That's Eastern Standard Time, of course. In Iraq it was already after 1:00 a.m. on the morning of January 17. I thought that bit of information was important. Just quoting the date alone doesn't seem very professional in my book, sir."

Arline's blood began to boil, and she nearly jumped up from her seat. She wanted so desperately to tell Stewart what Fred was doing, but instead, she clenched her teeth and forced herself to remain calm. *Jason had better get back here quick,* she thought. *And his idea had better be good.*

Fred went on to make his second and third questions look even easier than the first, while Arline managed to answer only one of the two correctly. By the time she was asked her fourth question, she was wondering if Jason would ever return.

"Your question this time," Nelson began, "concerns a man who changed the course of American history. His name was Charles J. Guiteau. Tell us what you know about the man, Arline. What major part did he play in changing our history, and what was the date the event occurred."

Arline felt her palms go sweaty. A huge lump formed in her throat. Even though the name sounded familiar, she couldn't put an event with it. And she knew from the smile on Fred's face that he was receiving the vital information over his hidden receiver.

* * *

Jason was cheerful as he entered Gus's office. "Good morning, Maggie," he greeted Gus's secretary. "How's your day going?"

Maggie smiled. "I think things are better for me right now than they are for you. I'd sure hate to be the one playing Cupid for Bruce."

"You know about my project, then?"

"I've been keeping close tabs on you, and unless I miss my guess, you're here to ask my help with Arline's panel interview."

Jason laughed. "That's it exactly, Maggie. No wonder old Gus always manages to keep his head above water. With you on his side, he couldn't fail if he wanted to."

Maggie gave Jason an affectionate look. "Thanks, Jason, that's a nice compliment. But I'm not sure I can help you out with your problem this time. You know I'm bound by rules that won't allow me to give Arline any answers that she doesn't already know for herself."

Jason didn't seem concerned. "I know that," he said, "but there's nothing against you preventing the other side from cheating, is there?"

"What is it you have in mind, Jason?" Maggie asked.

"This computer of yours is pretty powerful, isn't it?"

Maggie beamed proudly. "It's the best in the universe. With this little gem I can do unbelievable things."

"Like jamming the computer Fred Goodson is using to get the answers for himself?"

"Oh, yes, Jason," Maggie chuckled. "I can do that. And the best part is, it's perfectly legal. I won't be breaking any rules."

"How long will it take you to get set up?" Jason asked anxiously.

"It'll take less time than it took you to ask that question. Watch this." Maggie punched in a few keystroke commands and leaned back with a complacent smile. "That's it," she said. "Fred is in for a big surprise the next time his sneaky cousin touches his computer."

"Thanks, Maggie." Jason sighed with relief. "If I wasn't a happily married man, I'd kiss you."

"A simple thank-you will do nicely," Maggie chuckled.

* * *

"Hi, Arline, I'm back."

At the sight of Jason, Arline gave a sigh of relief. "I hope you brought the cavalry like you promised," she whispered. "I'm being buried here. I can't for the life of me remember who Charles Guiteau is. I'm sure I know; it's just that I can't pull it up right now."

"I can't tell you the answer, Arline. It's against the rules. But it might not hurt if I mention speaking to the man Charles murdered. Just a few weeks ago he dropped in for dinner at the Paradise Palace, where I work as head chef."

"President James B. Garfield!" Arline shouted out as Jason's hint turned on the light. "Charles Guiteau assassinated President Garfield! in May—no, it was in June 1881.

"That's right!" Nelson said, actually showing a hint of excitement.

"Way to go, Arline!" came Jason's added encouragement.

"Thanks, Jason," Arline whispered. "But don't give me any more hints. If I can't beat this man honestly, then I'll just have to lose. I refuse to sink to his level of integrity. Or lack of integrity would be a better way of saying it."

"Don't worry, Arline. Old Fred won't be cheating any more. He doesn't know that yet, but he will very shortly now."

"Well, Fred?" Nelson asked. "You seem to like adding to Arline's answers. Do you have anything more to add this time?"

"I do, sir. Charles killed the president with a butcher knife taken from the restaurant where they were dining at the time. Garfield died instantly from a punctured heart. Charles escaped and was never heard from again. Any schoolboy should know that part of the story. But then Arline was never a schoolboy, was she?"

Nelson removed his glasses and stared at Fred. "I have no idea where you came up with your information, young man," he grumbled. "But it's incorrect."

Fred laughed confidently. "Incorrect? Ha! Just check it out for yourself. It's all there in the encyclopedia."

"I just happen to have a copy of the article on the assassination from Compton's Interactive Encyclopedia," Nelson said, holding up the article for everyone to see. "The truth is, the assassination took place in the Pennsylvania Railroad Station in Washington, D.C. The president was struck with two shots from a revolver. He was hit in the arm and in the back near the spine. He didn't die until the following September. On June 30, 1882, a little over a year after the assassination, Charles Guiteau was hanged."

"Yeeooow!" Fred screamed. Everyone in the room watched in confusion as Fred quickly pulled a smoldering device from his inside coat pocket. After a brief but frantic struggle to dislodge it from a pair of electrical wires attached to his glasses, he tossed it to the floor in a heap of smoking electronic components and wires.

The room was silent as Stewart Carson slowly rose from his chair and crossed the room to stand before Fred, who wore a befuddled stare on his face. Carson looked down at the smoking object, and then at Fred. "Is this what I think it is, Fred?"

Fred's shoulders slumped. "Please, Mr. Carson," he began. "I can explain. You were about to make a terrible mistake, and I had to be sure it didn't happen. If Arline were to do better than me in this contest, you would have no choice but to give her the television show. I know her ratings are temporarily up because of this angel gimmick and all. But you know as well as I do that once the gimmick dies out, your new televised talk show will need a man to keep its popularity going. It's a man's world out there, and a woman can't possibly do the job on his level. I just wanted to make things easier for you by showing this panel you chose the right person when you gave me the job."

Every eye in the room turned to Stewart to see his reaction. The silence seemed interminable.

"Clean out your desk," he said in a quiet but commanding voice. "You have ten minutes to get out of this building. And I never want to see your face in here again. Is that understood?"

Fred stared at the smoldering receiver on the floor. Slowly he rose from his seat, and his eyes shifted past Stewart to Arline, and then back to his former boss.

"You haven't heard the last of me!" he said in a low voice. "I'll be back. And I'll show the lot of you what kind of mistake you're making in hiring Arline Wilson for this job." Then, with an angry obscenity, he stormed out of the room.

"Well, Arline," Stewart said, after a moment to recover from Fred's angry departure. "It looks like you have the job. That is, if you still want it."

"Oh, yes, sir. I do want the job."

"Very well, then. It's yours. I figure it will take three weeks to get everything set up. I'd like to have you leave your radio show now and take some time off to relax. Once the new show begins, it's going to be all work and no play. I hope you understand, the angel gimmick stays. We're still receiving phone calls on it. All of them positive, I might add."

Taken aback by the thought of leaving her radio show so soon, Arline was quick to ask, "Are you sure I should give up my show now? It wouldn't be that much trouble for me to hold onto it another couple of weeks."

"No. I'd really rather have you take some time off to relax a bit before the show begins. The first few days will make a big contribution to its success or failure, and I'd like to have you in top form. One other thing I'd like to have you do is set yourself up with a good-sized wardrobe before you begin. I'll have my secretary cut you a check for $5,000. You can do your own shopping. I completely trust your taste in what to wear in front of the camera. Do you have a problem with any of this?"

Arline found it difficult to speak. "You—You're giving me $5,000 for a new wardrobe and asking if I have a problem with it? You must be kidding. Shopping is my favorite pastime in the whole world. I'd rather shop than eat."

Stewart smiled. "Good, then you can enjoy your time away from work and set up your wardrobe as well. Plan on reporting to my office three weeks from today. I'll have the new contract ready for you to look over at that time. I need to work out a few details on your new salary, but I think you'll be happy with my offer. Now, are there any questions?"

"I don't think so." Arline's face showed a mixture of bewilderment and ecstasy. "It looks like you've taken care of everything, and you're certainly being generous."

"Fine, then. I'll see you in three weeks, and good luck."

"Thank you, Mr. Carson," Arline whispered as he led the panel of judges from the room. "And thank you, too, Jason," she added when the door shut behind them, leaving Arline and Jason alone in the room.

"Want to hear a story?" Jason asked, smiling.

Arline smiled back. "What kind of story?"

"It's about a young man named Arnold Bradford." At the familiar name, Arline turned her full attention to Jason.

"When Arnold was a freshman in high school," Jason began, "he was the butt of every cruel prank imaginable—probably because he stood barely five foot two and weighed only ninety pounds. It took raw courage for the kid to even show up at school in the mornings, but somehow he did it. One day at a school assembly, some of the older boys tricked Arnold into standing in front of the whole school and telling everyone about his first kiss. The problem was, Arnold had never been kissed. Unless you count his mother, that is. The guys who got him to the podium knew that. And for the most part, so did the rest of the student body.

"The auditorium broke into uproarious laughter and jeering. Everyone joined in. Everyone, that is, except for one of the prettiest and most popular young women in the school. The place fell dead silent as she stood and walked to the stage next to Arnold. 'He won't tell you,' she said. 'He's afraid of embarrassing me because I'm a senior and he's only a freshman. I'm not embarrassed to tell you, though. It was only last week when Arnold brought me home after a date at the movies. It wasn't my first kiss, but it was his. Arnold may not look much like a tiger, but watch out when you get alone with him, girls.' With that, this young lady kissed Arnold right there in front of them all. Not only did the auditorium break into stunned applause, Arnold Bradford became a school hero. He never missed a school dance in his four years of high school. The girls fought to go out with him. He later went on to play in a rock group and married the lead singer."

Arline stood in awe, listening to Jason's story. "You really are an angel," she gasped. "Either that, or you're a pretty darn good detective."

"I'm no detective," Jason assured her. "Sam told me the story herself. But it didn't come cheap. It cost several of my own most guarded secrets."

"What about the name?" Arline pressed. "If Sam really told you the story, she would have told you the name."

Jason smiled and continued his report. "After the school assembly broke up, Arnold wanted to give something to Sam to show his appreciation. The only thing he had with him was a Snickers candy bar, and so that became his gift of gratitude. Sam was so touched by the thoughtfulness of the gift, she refused to eat the candy bar. It remained in her mother's freezer for more than two years before she finally threw it out. From the day she kissed Arnold, you started calling her Snickers whenever you wanted to rile her. She hated the name, and you knew it. But that didn't stop you from using it. Oh, and by the way—" Jason added for additional proof of his case "—the two of you both ate frozen yogurt that day at the mall. Chocolate yogurt, and it was your treat."

Arline caught her breath and swallowed hard. "You're absolutely right," she admitted. "Snickers was the pet name I sometimes called Sam. You even got the part about the yogurt right. Jason Hackett, I don't know what to make of you. Just one thing bothers me, though. If you did get this information from Sam, why did you take so long coming back?"

"Because Sam refused to open up on the subject until this morning. Then, for some reason, she just felt like talking about it. I have no idea why she chose this morning to tell me the story, but I'm glad it worked out that way. It allowed me to get back just in time to learn of Fred's plan to rig the contest."

"Yeah," Arline agreed with a sigh. "I have to admit I'm glad you chose the time you did to show up. Otherwise, I'd be the one crying in my soda instead of Fred. I'm not sure how you managed your little trick of burning up his radio device, but I owe you a big one for doing it."

"I'll be glad to explain it to you sometime," Jason chuckled. "But for now let's keep our priorities in order. You are convinced I'm an angel now, aren't you?"

Arline looked thoughtful. "Well, I'm not a hundred percent sure you're an angel, Jason, although I am sure you're no ordinary man. Still, you could be some sort of hologram. I suppose you might even be nothing more than a short circuit in my imagination."

"Arline!" Jason exploded. "How can you possibly doubt me by this time? I've done everything you asked of me to give you your proof, haven't I?"

Yes, Arline agreed in her own mind. *He has done everything I asked. And he's come up with all the right answers. How else could he have known those things but to have learned them from Sam? And his story fits perfectly with my last conversation with Sam, when she tried to tell me she was in love with a ghost.*

"Answer one question for me," she replied. "You refer to yourself as an angel. Sam called you a ghost. What's the difference between the two?"

"Big difference," Jason responded insistently. "Ghosts are imaginary characters who frighten people for no reason other than their own pleasure. I've never tried to frighten anyone in my life, other than Bruce Vincent. I did try to shake him up once." Jason had to chuckle as he remembered the event. "But even then it was only a simple prank. I didn't make an occupation out of frightening the man."

"What about Casper? He's supposedly a friendly ghost."

"Come on, Arline! Just call me an angel, all right? And I'll call you a talk show hostess instead of a disc jockey. Deal?"

Arline glanced at her watch. "I'll have to think on that one, but I will make you another deal. I need to get home right now. Why don't you come along for the ride and use the time to tell me the whole story of your courtship with Sam. I have to admit my curiosity is about to explode. And it can't hurt your cause to tell the whole story."

CHAPTER SIX

The drive home took a little over half an hour—just enough time for Jason to relate the story of Gus's typo and the years of discouragement that followed until destiny was eventually restored to its designed course. He told of being born more than thirty years ahead of his time, and how Samantha was a mere child at the time of his death. Line by line he laid out the whole story, including his courtship of Samantha and her ultimate decision to join him on the far side of forever. By the time Arline pulled her Toyota into the driveway of her home, she was ready to believe in angels. Not only in Jason, but in Samantha as well.

"Your story certainly clears up a lot of things for me," she admitted, as the two of them walked from the car to her house. "For the first time I understand what Sam was trying to tell me that day at the mall. She really was in love with a ghost."

"Arline!"

"All right, she was in love with an angel," Arline corrected herself. "And I have to admit, it's kind of nice knowing Sam is still around. Especially if she's as happy as you say she is."

"She's happy, all right. But she won't be if anything prevents Bruce from being married on schedule. Her contract guarantees the marriage, and if anything goes wrong . . ."

"Say no more, Jason. Knowing Sam like I do, I understand what you mean. The one thing I don't understand, though, is why you're dealing with me. If Bruce is the reason you're here, why not deal directly with him?"

Jason shook his head in disgust. "That, Arline, is a very good question. Whenever an angel is sent here on an assignment, there are certain rules attached. In my case, I'm allowed to be seen and heard by one person alone. According to Gus's original plan, that person was supposed to be Bruce. Something went wrong. Neither of us know for sure what happened. But whatever it was, you ended up my only contact on this side. There's nothing any of us can do but make the best of the situation."

Arline looked surprised. "You mean even angels make mistakes? I always assumed if angels really existed, they'd have everything under control at all times. At least in the movies it works that way."

"Hollywood angels are a joke," Jason scoffed. "Those guys know as much about angels as I know about playing the harp"

"You don't play a harp, either?"

In spite of himself, Jason broke out laughing. "No, Arline," he said patiently. "I don't play the harp, I don't have wings, and I'm not immune from making mistakes. Like I told you before, I'm nothing more than a man who has passed over the line into the next dimension."

Arline shook her head as if to clear away all the confusing information she was learning. "This comes as a rather staggering thought, Jason. Even though I never gave much consideration to angels appearing on my side, I did naturally assume they existed where you come from. And I sort of hoped they had things better in hand than you tell me they do."

"Things are in hand on my side, Arline," Jason tried desperately to explain, as they stepped up to the front door and Arline took out her key. "It's just that angels aren't the ones in charge. We're the bottom rung on the ladder, so to speak. It's the higher authorities who keep everything in order."

"You have higher authorities over there?"

"That's right. And they never make mistakes."

Arline unlocked her door and stepped inside. Jason followed.

"Okay," she said, "if they never make mistakes, explain how Gus's typo managed to get through the net."

"Oh, boy," Jason said, wiping his brow with one hand, "I'm limited to what I can tell you about what goes on over there, but I'll say this. First, Gus isn't an angel like Sam and me. Centuries ago he was, but now he's advanced way beyond that point. He's not limited by many of the things I am. For instance, if you were to shake hands with Gus, you would feel it. Or if he showed up in a crowd, everyone would be able to see him. He even has the power to control certain elements of nature that might seem impossible.

"But even so, he's still not one of the higher authorities, and he's still subject to making mistakes now and then. The higher authorities could have prevented him from making that error, but they didn't. They left Gus with his own agency, but he's still responsible for his actions." Jason paused, then added, "The higher authorities never force a person to do anything."

"I think I'm beginning to get the picture," Arline said thoughtfully, as she tossed her purse to the sofa and headed to the kitchen. "Gus made the mistake, so they let him undo his own problem. And now he's made another mistake."

Jason followed her. "Well, sort of. This time it wasn't so much of a mistake as it was not putting enough effort into getting the job done right the first time. He just assumed that all he had to do was get Bruce and Jenice together, and nature would take care of the rest. It didn't work that way, and so I'm down here on this assignment."

Now it was Arline's turn to laugh. "And if you don't get Bruce a wife, you have to answer to Sam, right?"

"That's it, in a nutshell," Jason sighed.

"You really do need my help, don't you?"

"Does a fish need water?"

"I thought Bruce and Jenice had already set the date. I'm sure she's wearing his ring."

"Not any more. She gave the ring back to him a week ago."

Arline stopped in her tracks and looked back at Jason. "She gave his ring back? The marriage is off, then?"

"Not completely," Jason replied. "It seems Jenice Anderson is the kind of woman who loves adventure. It's not that she doesn't care for Bruce, it's just that she wants him to make some drastic changes in his lifestyle if she's going to marry him."

Arline opened the dishwasher. "What kind of changes?" she asked as she began to put the clean dishes back into the cupboard. "Somehow I can't picture Bruce ever becoming the adventuresome type."

"Frankly, I can't picture the wimp as adventuresome, either,"

Jason agreed. "But Jenice is putting some heavy pressure on the guy to become just that. She's given him until April 15th to re-propose to her. Only this time, he has to do it her way."

"Her way?" Arline looked over her shoulder at Jason and gave him a questioning look. "Just what is her way? Knowing Bruce, if it's anything harder than getting him into a McDonald's restaurant to do the asking, he's in big trouble."

Jason paused for effect, then announced, "She wants him to skydive onto a beach where she'll be waiting."

"Skydive?" Arline choked. "She wants Bruce to jump out of an airplane? She might as well ask him to paint the moon blue and give it to her on a silver platter."

"Now do you see why I need your help?" Jason said glumly.

"I admit, you do have a problem. How bad will it be if the marriage doesn't come off? Other than having to face Sam, I mean."

"Bad, I'm afraid. Gus is facing the discipline of the higher authorities this time. They were willing to overlook his typo. But now, this is a second mistake on the same contract. The contract should have been closed out long ago, and now there's a threat of more delays. This time Gus is in big trouble. Unless Bruce is married by the deadline, the contract remains open."

A worried look crossed Arline's face. "The contract will remain open?" she asked. "How will that affect you and Sam? Wasn't the part about Bruce being married within a year only a small add-on to the overall contract that basically concerned just the two of you?"

Jason nodded in partial agreement to Arline's conclusion. "The contract does basically concern Sam and me," he explained. "And, fortunately for us, the higher authorities have agreed to allow the rest of the contract to continue in effect, even if the 'Bruce clause' does remain open. It's Gus who's in trouble here. Unless the complete contract is closed out on time, the higher authorities have expressed their intent to remove Gus from his job as Special Conditions Coordinator. He'll be reassigned as the Manager of Weather Control in the Sahara Desert."

Arline wrinkled her nose. "That does sound serious," she agreed.

"Gus and I have been through a lot together," Jason explained. "This time he needs me. It was the other way around for more than

twenty years, and he never let me down. I just can't bring myself to
let him down now."

With the dishes put away, Arline stepped to the refrigerator and
pulled open the door. "I'm dying for something to drink," she said.
"I'd offer you something, but . . ."

"I'm fine, Arline. Go ahead and have something yourself."

"I got a better idea," came an unexpected voice from behind. "I'll
furnish the drinks, if the three of us can sit down and talk."

Arline whirled around to face this new intruder. "What are you
doing in my house?!" she exploded.

"It's okay, Arline," Jason quickly intervened. "This is my friend
Gus. You never know when he's liable to show up."

Arline stared at the strange little man who held a tray with a large
bottle of bright blue liquid and three glasses. "You're Gus
Winkelbury?" she asked in astonishment. "The one responsible for
the typo in Sam and Jason's contract?"

"I see Jason's been busy spreadin' his side of the story. I hope he
didn't paint too bad a picture of me. I'm sorry ta barge in on ya like
this, Arline, but somethin's come up."

"Something's come up?" Jason groaned. "What now? I'd say we've
already had enough surprises for one assignment, wouldn't you?"

"Hey, pal, take it easy. It's not somethin' we can't handle. It's just
another little setback, that's all."

"Another setback? I'm afraid to ask what this one is."

"Whaddya say the three of us sit down and have a cold drink?
There's no need gettin' upset. We can talk this over like adults."

Gus set the glasses on Arline's table and filled two of them from
the bottle. The third glass just seemed to fill itself, as if from an
unseen hand. "This one is Jason's," Gus explained. "The other two
are ours. Sit down and try some, Arline. I think yer gonna like it."

Arline took a deep breath, closed the door to her refrigerator, and
sat down cautiously in front of the drink Gus had poured. "What is
it?" she asked.

"It's a concoction Jason came up with." Gus explained. "He's
been servin' it at the Paradise Palace where he works as a chef. A job I
got for him, by the way," he added with a meaningful look aimed at
Jason.

Arline took a sip of the drink. "Wow!" she exclaimed. "This is great. You invented it yourself, Jason?"

"Yes, Arline. It's one of my creations. But if you'll excuse my impatience, I'd like an explanation of why Gus is here. I have this feeling in the pit of my stomach that I'm not going to like what I hear."

"I think ya better sit down, Jase," Gus said, pulling out a chair for him. "Yer probably right about not likin' what I'm gonna tell ya."

Jason refused the chair and remained standing. "I remember the last time you asked me to sit down for one of your explanations."

"Okay, pal, suit yerself. It looks like yer gonna have ta finish this assignment without my help. It seems the higher authorities have picked this time ta call a Multi-Universe Conference. They've never invited me ta one of these things before, but—"

"What?!" Jason bellowed. "You're chasing off to some conference and leaving me alone on an assignment that's probably impossible anyway? Aren't you forgetting something here, Gus? You're the one whose neck is on the chopping block, not mine. I think you'd better find a way to get out of this conference, unless you'd like to spend the next few hundred years on the Sahara Desert, that is."

"Come on, Jason, give me a break here, will ya? It's not like I planned ta leave ya on yer own with a project that means so much ta me personally. I got no choice. I found a message on my computer, not half an hour ago. My immediate presence is requested three galaxies from here. The worst part is, there's no tellin' how long these conferences will last. The bottom line is, my life is in yer hands, pal." He looked up at Jason, who ignored the pleading look in his eyes.

"Gus! Do you realize the magnitude of what you're dumping on me here? We only had a month approved in the beginning of this assignment. A week is gone already. That leaves me doing the impossible, without any of your extraterrestrial help, in only three short weeks. And I'm already handicapped by not being able to communicate directly with Bruce. Do you have any suggestions how I can get the job done, old friend?"

"As long as the two of you are using my kitchen table for your planning session," Arline broke in, "do you think it would be asking too much to be included in on the conversation? I know you want my help with the problem, but I just naturally assumed you would come up with the plan of how to go about it. Now, unless I've missed something here, you're saying there is no plan."

"What's the big deal?" Gus asked. "All ya have ta do is be Jason's translator, so he can get through ta Bruce. I'm sure between the two of you you'll come up with somethin' ta help the old boy get the girl."

"Oh, wonderful," Arline said sarcastically. "I'm supposed to approach a psychologist with the story I'm representing an angel that wants to use me as a medium to help get him married. I should be able to carry that one off with no trouble."

Gus looked uncomfortable. "Okay, so what I'm askin' isn't exactly easy. That don't mean it can't be done. With your talent for words and Jason's experience with Bruce, the two of you can pull it off." He turned his pleading look to Arline. "Ya hafta pull it off, or it's catastrophic for me."

Jason groaned in disgust. "You're depending on my former experience with Bruce? Get real, Gus, the guy hates me. And another thing, how are we supposed to make contact with Bruce in the first place? I just assumed you'd figure out a way for that to happen."

"It's already taken care of, Jason. Before I left the office I used my computer ta juggle Bruce's appointment calendar. Arline has an appointment with the old boy at ten o'clock Monday mornin'."

"What?" Arline gasped. "You have me on the books as one of his clients? You were pretty sure of yourself, weren't you, mister? What if I'd refused to help you? I still might refuse, you know."

"Ya hafta understand, Arline. I have this keen ability for judging a person's character. I'm never wrong. I had no doubt at all that you'd come through."

"Yeah, sure," Jason said irritably. "That's why I heard you giving Maggie the third degree on your chances of getting Arline's help. I'd say it was Maggie's judge of character that paved the way for you in this one, Gus."

Gus squirmed. "Maggie's opinion might have had somethin' ta do with it. But it worked out okay, didn't it? Ya will help me out here, won't ya, Arline?"

Arline sighed. "Yes, Gus. I'll help you out all I can. But you'd better know right up front that I'm not a miracle worker. If the success of this project depends on getting Bruce to jump out of an airplane, it just might be a bigger knot than I can tie."

* * *

"Good morning, Ms. Bates," Bruce said to his secretary as he stepped into the suite. "What time is my first appointment?"

"I'm sure it's not until eleven, Mr. Vincent," Marsha Bates answered, punching in a few commands on her computer. "But I'll check just to be sure." It took only seconds for the calendar to come up on the screen. "No, I was wrong," she said with a look of bewilderment. "I don't recall making this one at all. My memory must be slipping. Why does the name Arline Wilson seem so familiar to me? I'm sure she's not one of your former clients."

Bruce looked startled. "Arline Wilson has an appointment to see me?"

"Yes, sir. At ten o'clock."

"Arline was Samantha's good friend."

"Yes, that's right. I remember now. But I certainly don't remember making this appointment. I think I should cut back on the NutraSweet for a while."

She studied Bruce's face, then swiveled her chair to face him. "Something's bothering you, isn't it? I've noticed you seem a little down lately. Have you been ill?"

"No, Ms. Bates, I haven't been ill. What's bothering me is more serious than a simple virus, I'm afraid. It's Jenice. I fear I'm about to lose her. It seems she places more importance on climbing mountains than she does on marriage. She's given me an ultimatum." For a moment, Bruce looked too ill to speak, then he managed to choke out, "She wants me to parachute from an airplane onto an open stretch of beach, where she'll be waiting for me to propose to her again."

"But, Mr. Vincent, why would she want you to parachute from an airplane?" The secretary looked bewildered.

Bruce moved a hand to his head and brushed back his heavy dark hair. "It's my lifestyle," he answered, staring upward as though looking through the ceiling. "She has given me the choice of changing my lifestyle to suit her liking or to no longer be a part of her life. I don't know what I'm going to do, Ms. Bates. I thought my life had ended when I lost Samantha to that dreadful accident. Then, almost as though some unseen force had planned a way to keep me from losing my sanity, I met Jenice. It's true I've never had the strong feeling for Jenice I held for Samantha, but I do care a great deal for her. I've always been sure that in time I would learn to love her the way I loved Samantha. But now . . ."

"I'm so sorry," Mrs. Bates comforted him. "I wish there was something I could say."

Bruce's smile returned, this time a little warmer. "Thanks, Ms. Bates," he responded. "It helps knowing you care." Glancing at his watch, Bruce realized he had a few minutes before Arline's appointment. "I'll be in my office," he said, pushing open the door. "Buzz me when she arrives, will you?"

Closing the door behind him, Bruce stared at his elegant office and allowed thoughts of Samantha's last visit here to come vividly back to his mind. It was the day she had approached him about having his friend Philip Morgan check some old military records to learn if Jason Hackett was real or simply a fictional character made up by one of her fifth-grade students. Little did he imagine how the name Jason Hackett would come back to sting him in the months that followed.

"Samantha, darling," he had asked that day, "What are you doing here?"

"Do I need a special reason?" she had answered. "What's the matter, Bruce? Afraid I'll find you with another woman?"

Bruce released a long, slow sigh as he remembered becoming so uptight at her remark.

"Don't be silly," he had replied sharply. "You know perfectly well you're the only woman in my life."

Tears glistened in Bruce's eyes, something very uncommon for him, as he saw again the smile on her face as she playfully pushed him away.

"Lighten up, Bruce," she had laughed. "I was only making a joke."

After he had made a big issue about some subjects not being joked about, she had asked, "What am I ever going to do with you, Bruce? I can see I have my work cut out for me. You have no idea what life is really all about. I have to find a way to improve that stuffy attitude of yours. You need to learn that life is much too important to be taken so seriously."

Again and again these words echoed loudly through the roadways of his memory. They haunted him not only because Samantha had said them, but also because they were now being echoed by Jenice.

It's true, he admitted to himself painfully. *I do take life too seriously. I simply must learn to lighten up, or I shall have a second love torn from the pages of my life. If I can't find a way to become the man Jenice wants me to be, she'll be gone forever just as surely as Samantha is. Unless I can bring myself to parachute from an airplane in just three short weeks, my life will no longer be worth living. But how can I? Knowing myself as I do, I must admit it's pretty nearly impossible.*

Crossing the office, Bruce took a seat in his plush brown leather chair and swiveled around to look through the window behind his desk. More of Samantha's words returned as he remembered her seated here, looking at the city below.

"You really live a rough life," she had observed. *"Fine cars, luxurious houses, an office with a view like this. What would it be like?"*

What is it like, indeed? he pondered. *All of these things I have, and still happiness eludes me. I would gladly have traded them all for a lifetime with Samantha. And I'd trade them all now, just to share the rest of my life with Jenice.*

At that moment, he was interrupted by the sound of his intercom. "Your client is here, Mr. Vincent," Marsha's voice said cheerfully. "Shall I send her in?"

CHAPTER SEVEN

Stepping into the office, Arline immediately saw Bruce seated behind his huge mahogany desk. The last time she had seen Bruce was at Samantha's funeral. Seeing him now was like opening an old wound.

Nevertheless, as their eyes met she felt the beat of her heart sky-rocket. She had forgotten how handsome he was. Although he smiled at her, his smile didn't reach his eyes. Obviously, something was troubling him. This was even more evident by the tone of his voice as he called her by name.

"Arline, it's so good to see you, again." He remained seated as he spoke.

"Hello, Bruce," Arline responded, closing the door behind her. "It's good to see you, too. I'm glad to say you're looking better than you did the last time we met."

"You mean at the funeral?"

"Yes."

"That was a dreadful day for all of us. I try not to think of it often. I must say you look rather stunning yourself, Arline. That's a lovely dress you're wearing. Is it new?"

Arline was glad Bruce had chosen not to dwell on the subject of the funeral. She was also flattered by his compliment.

"Yes, Bruce, the dress is new. You should remember how much I love shopping." She smiled.

"How could I ever forget?" His reply came with a halfhearted chuckle. Rising to his feet, he crossed the room to meet Arline halfway. "I'm so glad you stopped in," he said, kissing the back of her hand. "What brings you here? Nothing serious, I trust."

Nothing serious? Arline laughed quietly to herself. *I'm here to help this angel standing next to me fill an assignment to get you married with-in the next four and a half months. Yes, I'd say that's just a little bit seri-ous. But—how am I going to approach the subject?*

"What brings me here, Bruce," she struggled, "is a little hard to explain."

"I don't understand, Arline. What could possibly bring you to see me that would be so hard to explain?"

"Whatever you do," Jason warned. "Don't mention me to Bruce. That would be the worst thing you could do. The guy hates me."

Ignoring Jason's remarks, Arline made the decision that a direct approach to the subject might be the best. It was a method that worked well on her talk show. Why wouldn't it work with Bruce? Gathering all her courage, she asked a pointed question. "Do you ever deal with people who claim to talk with angels, or perhaps ghosts, in your profession, Bruce?"

Bruce went pale. "Why would a question like that cross your mind, Arline?"

"I know about Samantha's ghost," she answered bluntly. "And the ghost, or angel if you prefer, is the reason I'm here now."

"I think we'd better sit down," Bruce stammered, pointing to one of two black leather chairs near his desk. Arline took the invitation and sat in the one nearest her. Bruce sat in the other. "Exactly what do you know about Samantha's ghost?" he asked guardedly.

"I'm telling you, Arline," Jason protested. "This is the wrong way to approach the problem. The wimp and I are not what you might call close friends. You'll drive him away for sure by bringing up my name."

"I know a great deal about the ghost," Arline explained. "Sam filled me in on him the last time I saw her alive."

Large beads of perspiration were forming on Bruce's brow by this time. "You have to understand, Arline," he explained. "Most psychol-ogists would shun the subject of ghosts like the plague. I can no longer do that. I know for certain Samantha did have a ghost haunt-ing her. In fact, at the risk of having you think me a little off plumb, I must say I strongly suspect her ghost had something to do with the accident that claimed her life."

Arline took a deep breath. "What would you say, Bruce, if I told you Jason Hackett was in this room right now, not more than two feet from where you're sitting?"

Gripped by a sudden look of terror, Bruce shot to his feet. "The ghost is in this room? Where is he?"

"Oh, boy," Jason said, rolling his eyes upward and throwing a hand to his forehead. "Here we go. You've done it now, Arline."

"He's standing right there, next to the corner of your desk," Arline replied. "He asked me to say 'Hi'."

"You mean you can see and hear him now? Like Samantha did before he killed her? Arline, we have to do something to protect you from him! He's liable to kill you, too!"

"No, Bruce, you've got the wrong idea about Jason. He's harmless, I assure you. He's not haunting either of us. In fact, he's here to do you a service if you'll allow him to."

"I don't believe you." Bruce quickly stepped to the side of his desk, at exactly the farthest distance from where Arline said Jason was standing. "He's not satisfied with Samantha's death. He wants us now!"

Arline stood and walked over next to Bruce. Taking him firmly by the arm, she led him back to his chair. "Sit down," she said. "We need to talk. I give you my word Jason means neither of us any harm. In fact, he told me just this morning how much he likes and admires you."

"Oh, pleeeeze!" Jason groaned. "I'd never say anything like that, Arline. As an angel, I'm duty bound to tell the truth at all times."

Bruce looked suspiciously toward the corner of the desk where Jason was standing. "I don't know, Arline," he said cautiously. "Trusting this ghost is a mistake. What happened to Samantha could easily happen to us as well."

Arline spoke gently. "I know how strange this is for you because I'm only beginning to grasp the meaning of it all myself. You're wrong about Jason taking Sam's life. It was Sam's own decision to move on into the next dimension when she did. Jason had nothing to do with it, unless you hold him guilty for making Sam fall in love with him."

"That's nonsense!" Bruce protested. "Samantha was in love with me. It was to have been our wedding day. Instead, because of this ghost—"

Arline shook her head. "I'm sorry to tell you this, Bruce, but even though Sam was very fond of you, it was Jason she was in love with. She agreed to marry you only because there seemed no way of ever having a life with him."

Bruce looked pained. "I don't believe this. The ghost is obviously lying."

Arline leaned forward and took Bruce's hand. "I didn't believe him either until he told me some things that only Sam could have known," she said. "He *is* telling the truth, Bruce. I'm sure of that now. Which brings us back to the reason we're here. Will you give me the chance to explain it to you?"

"I—I suppose so. But I still don't trust that ghost."

Arline pulled her chair around so it was just in front of Bruce's. Taking Bruce's hand again, she went on with her explanation. "Sam knew how badly it would hurt you when she stepped out of your life. She couldn't bring herself to leave you without knowing you would be all right. With this in mind, before she consented to go with Jason into his dimension, she pressured Gus into agreeing to help you find someone to take her place."

Bruce slunk back in his chair. "Gus?" he moaned. "Samantha mentioned Gus several times, but I never did learn who he's supposed to be."

"Gus is—well for want of a better word, I'll call him another angel. You see, Jason was forced to remain here on this side for more than twenty years after his own death. When we have more time, I'll explain why that was necessary. Anyway, Gus was Jason's go-between, from one world to the other during all that time."

"This is bringing back too many painful memories," Bruce gasped weakly. "Why won't this ghost just go away and leave me alone?"

"Believe me, Bruce," Jason fumed. "You don't wish that any more than I do myself. There are a lot more pleasant things I could be doing with my time than baby-sitting a wimp."

"Will you stop complaining!" Arline snapped. "This is your assignment, you know. For two cents I'd walk out that door and leave you to figure it out without my help."

Bruce looked at her blankly. "What assignment do you mean?"

"I wasn't talking to you, Bruce," Arline snapped. "I was talking to Jason."

Bruce buried his face deep in both hands. "Oh, no," he groaned. "Do I have to go through this again?"

Exasperated, Arline stood up and walked toward Bruce's desk. She picked up the magazine he had been holding when she and Jason first entered his office. "When did you develop an interest in skydiving, Bruce," she asked. Then before he could speak, she added, "Let me guess. It was since your last date with Jenice Anderson, when you took her to dinner at the Hunter's Cottage, right?"

"How could you know about . . . ? Good grief! That pesky ghost has been spying on my dates again just as he did with Samantha."

"I wasn't spying," Jason defended himself. "I was simply doing some research for my assignment. I'd never even met Jenice before, and I needed to learn a little about her. Heaven forbid she ever finds out I was a party to helping Bruce ruin her life."

"Jason says he wasn't spying on you," Arline reported to Bruce. "The one dinner date is the only time he was around while you were with Jenice. He was only there because he wants to help you."

"He wants to help me?" Bruce scoffed. "Ha, that's preposterous! That ghost would never do anything to help me, Arline."

"What about the time he saved your life, when the armed men were robbing your house? Didn't he help you then?" Arline reminded Bruce.

Bruce's face grew pale. "How did you know about that?" he whimpered.

"Jason told me, when he was relating the rest of his story."

Bruce rose and walked to the window behind his desk, where he stood looking out across the busy city streets below. "I suppose he did save my life," he admitted. "Did he tell you—everything about Jenice and me?"

"Are you referring to her ultimatum?"

He nodded soberly. Arline's face was sympathetic as she continued, "I'm sure you'd have to love her very much to consider jumping out of an airplane. You must be pretty torn up over this, Bruce. Unless I miss my guess, your insides are tearing apart right about now."

"Yes, that pretty well describes the feeling," Bruce confessed, still looking out the window. "I lost Samantha, and now I'm about to lose Jenice unless I can learn how to become more daring. Quite frankly, the thought frightens me to death."

Arline moved close to Bruce and put her hand on his arm. As he turned to look at her, she said softly, "That's the reason Jason and I are here, Bruce. You didn't meet Jenice Anderson by accident. It was all part of the contract Sam pressured Gus into signing. Gus used his computer to come up with Jenice's name, then he set it up for the two of you to meet at Sam's funeral. For a while everything seemed to be moving along on schedule. The trouble is, even with the help of Gus's computer, he still underestimated Jenice's desire for a life of adventure. And unfortunately, Bruce, you don't measure up to her expectations. Not for the moment, at least. So in order to get things on track, Jason and I are here to help you."

Bruce didn't look encouraged by Arline's words. "You're here to play matchmaker for two misfits, is that it?"

Arline didn't take offense. "That's putting it a little harsh, but you have the general idea."

"I'm the psychologist. It's my place to help others with their problems. Not vice versa," Bruce argued.

"I can't speak for Jason's qualifications, but in case you haven't noticed, Bruce, I'm a woman." Arline smiled. "I come a lot closer to understanding how Jenice thinks, and feels, than you do. But of course if you don't want my help, I can always leave." She turned and took a few steps, as if intending to leave.

"No! Please don't leave," Bruce begged her. "This is very difficult for me, Arline. Especially since the ghost is involved. But I don't want to lose Jenice. If you can help me, then please, I'll do whatever you say."

"All right then, I'll do what I can. But—" she warned, "you have to promise not to give me any trouble when I ask you to do something you might not like."

Bruce was silent for a few long minutes. "Be honest with me, Arline," he said at last. "You've known me for some time now. Do you think there's a chance I can learn to be more daring? There's so very little time, you understand."

Arline bit her lip and struggled for the right words to answer Bruce. To be completely honest, she wasn't at all sure Bruce could change. Still, she owed it to Samantha to give it her best shot.

"I think, Bruce," she said after considering it for a moment, "that you have the power within you to make the change. But only if you want to badly enough. It will require a great deal of effort on your part. I'm willing to give you all the help I can, if you're sure you want my help."

Bruce sighed. "Yes, I do want your help. Hard as it is for me to ask, I do want your help. Where do we start?"

CHAPTER EIGHT

Fred Goodson switched off the engine to his white Ford pickup truck and dropped the keys into his shirt pocket. Then he rubbed his chin as he stared at the old but neatly kept house trailer parked under the shade of two massive cottonwood trees. He hadn't been to see Uncle Elmo for years, since about the time he'd started working for Stewart Carson.

Fred closed his eyes and thought of his former boss. When Stewart had told him about the television show he had planned, Fred could have shouted with joy. He knew with his looks and charisma, he'd be a hit with a live audience in front of a camera.

Then, like a slap in the face, Stewart had given the job to Arline. What greater insult could the man have thrown at Fred than to choose a woman for the job that should have been his?

Stepping out of his truck, Fred heard the hooting of an owl over the gurgling sound of Henderson Creek, which ran swiftly along its course just behind Elmo's trailer. A few crickets chirped their message of affection in time with the tapping of an energetic woodpecker among the rustling leaves of the cottonwood trees. All the sounds of a busy city, so familiar to Fred, were noticeably missing here at the base of Henderson Mountain. That was not surprising, though, since the nearest sign of civilization was Highline Road, nearly ten miles to the south.

Most pleasant of all, to Fred's ears, was not the sounds he was hearing, but the one sound that was missing: the slow, deep barking of Elmo's friendly old bloodhound, Rastus. Fred held a mild hatred for most dogs, but Rastus was different. Fred hated Rastus with a passion.

Maybe the old dog had finally gone on to chase the spirits of departed jackrabbits in bloodhound heaven, wherever that might be,

Fred thought. And good riddance. With a smile, Fred walked briskly toward the trailer.

He was nearly there when he heard the first friendly sound emitting from Rastus's big throat. With swishing tail and that infernal dog smile he always wore, Rastus appeared at a full gallop from a nearby gully.

"No, Rastus, back!" Fred shouted in vain, as the big dog bounded straight for him. In an instant, Fred was on the ground with Rastus standing over him drooling happily in his face and filling his nostrils with dog breath.

"Uncle Elmo! Help!" Fred cried out. "Get this beast off me!"

"What in tarnation's going on out here?" A stubby little man in striped overalls and matching engineer's cap pushed the screen door to one side and ambled toward man and dog. "Is that you, Fred? For crying in the bucket, son, don't you know better than to get old Rastus all worked up like that? You know how excited he gets when a visitor happens by the place."

"Just get him off me, Uncle Elmo," Fred pleaded. "He can get friendly with a beaver or some other animal that appreciates him more than I do."

"Go on, boy," Elmo said, motioning for the hound to move away from Fred. "This city slicker's not one to want your affection, fella." Rastus immediately moved a few feet away from Fred, shook his head slowly, and let out a low friendly growl.

"Well, are you just going to lay there in the dirt, boy?" Elmo asked, as he looked down on his nephew. "Or are you going to stand up and tell me what brings you out my way?"

Keeping a watchful eye on Rastus, Fred managed to get to his feet while wiping his face with a handkerchief taken from his pocket. "How much longer is that old hound going to live?" he asked in disgust. "He must be over a hundred in dog years by now."

"You leave old Rastus be, Fred. He's got plenty of squirrel-chasing years left in him yet. He's a whole lot like me, still useful as all getout but unwanted by a world that's forgot what we're useful for. Now are you going to tell me what you're doing out here or not? I know it would take something pretty earthshaking to bring you out my way."

Fred crammed the damp handkerchief back in his pocket while

brushing himself off with the other hand. "I'm here to offer you some 'up-front cash' business, if the old Henderson Railroad is still in running condition. It is still workable, I assume?"

"Ha! Come on back here and have a look for yourself." Elmo started off in the direction of an old wooden bridge over the creek just behind his trailer.

With one eye on Rastus, who was still panting with joy and wagging his long scraggly tail, Fred hurried to catch up to his uncle. Elmo moved at a pace much faster than Fred was accustomed to, and the younger man was soon breathing heavily from the effort of keeping up. Once over the bridge, the two men made their way toward a large red building several hundred feet behind the trailer. By the time Fred reached the building, Elmo had swung open one of two large swinging doors. There stood a shiny red steam engine, coal car, two passenger coaches, and a matching red caboose.

Fred gasped in amazement at the condition of the old Engine 707. It looked as shiny and spotless as it had the day it had made its final run up to Henderson Lodge some twenty years before. Fred had been a passenger on that historic run, as had the rest of Elmo's family. That day had marked the end of an era. For years the train had made two round trips a day, carrying tenants to and from the lodge. Even though the business was still thriving at the time of Shad Henderson's death, his two sons were not of a mind to keep it going. They had plenty of money coming in from their father's other, less-complicated enterprises.

But Shad Henderson's will had stipulated that the railroad and lodge be kept exactly as he had constructed them and made sure funds were appropriated for the task. Elmo Spatford was to remain in charge of the operation for as long as he lived. It was evident from the appearance of the old train that Elmo took the task seriously.

"I'm impressed," Fred said between gulps for air to his burning lungs. "Does it still run as good as it looks?"

"Does a gopher eat carrots? The sun never rose on a day when old 707 ran any better than it does now. I still take her up to the lodge two or three times a week. It's a little more lonesome than it used to be, but it's still a doggone beautiful thirty-five mile ride. Takes an hour each way, just like always."

"Is the railroad line still the only way up to the old lodge? I mean, they haven't put in a road or anything, have they?"

Elmo eyed Fred suspiciously. "Nothing's changed," he replied, lowering his voice a pitch or two. "The only way up to the lodge, other than old 707 here, would be by one of them fancy helicopter gadgets they use nowadays. Now, tell me, why would a young whippersnapper like you be suddenly interested in these things, anyway?"

Fred tried to speak casually. "Like I said before, Uncle Elmo, I have some potential customers for you. I know your railroad isn't open to the public any more, but I was hoping you could accommodate some friends of mine as a personal favor to me. Do you think we could work something out?"

Elmo narrowed his eyes in thought. "Well, now, son, that all depends on what you have in mind. Would you like to spell it out for me?"

Fred drew in one last deep breath and groped for the right way to put his offer. "I have these friends, you see. And—well, this one friend wants to play a practical joke on his girlfriend."

"What kind of practical joke?"

"He . . . uh . . . wants to propose to her. Yes, that's it. He wants to pretend like she's been kidnapped to the old Henderson Lodge. Then, right in the middle of the joke, he'll suddenly show up and propose to her. I'm—I mean, *he's* willing to pay . . . say . . . a thousand dollars for your services. All you have to do is run our party up to the lodge, leave us there a couple of days, then pick us up again. How about it, Uncle Elmo? Will you help me out here?"

"You say this fellow wants to ask his girlfriend to marry him?" Elmo snorted. "Why not just buy her a dozen roses and propose in some moonlit park?"

"No, you don't understand." Fred paused to wipe the sweat from his face. "He . . . he wants to propose to her in a special way. It can't be some run-of-the-mill thing like a moonlit park. The kidnap gimmick is original. It has class. Come on, Uncle Elmo, be a sport. I know you can use the thousand dollars."

Elmo shook his head definitely. "Nope. I don't need the money. Old Henderson left me well enough off in that bracket. If I decide to help you out with your prank, it's just as a favor. I have to admit, though, it sure would be nice to have some living, breathing people on the train again just once before I die. When would you be wanting to make the trip?"

"I'm not sure of the exact date yet. It should be between two and three weeks, depending on how long it takes to make all the other arrangements. It won't be any longer than three weeks, I'm sure of that much. What do you say? Will you do it?"

"By howdy," Elmo said, slamming a clenched fist into an open palm, "I think I'll just do that. I'll spend some time cleaning up a few rooms at the lodge. Not that they need much cleaning, mind you. I stay pretty well up on that sort of thing. Maybe just a touch-up here and there is all they need."

"How much notice do you need for an exact time and date?"

"Don't need any notice. I won't be going nowhere. When you and your friends show up, it'll take less than ten minutes to fire up old 707 and get her on the rails."

CHAPTER NINE

"But, Arline, why are you doing this to me? I'm perfectly happy with the clothes I wear, and I see no possible connection between my clothes and parachuting from an airplane."

Arline moved rapidly through articles on the circular clothes rack, looking for just the right sport shirt to go with the pair of tan Haggar slacks she had picked out moments earlier.

"Don't argue with me, Bruce. I know what I'm doing," she said, without taking her eyes from the clothes rack. "I've never seen you wear anything exciting. If you're not in that outdated gray pinstriped suit, you're dressed in something drab enough to put a Tasmanian devil to sleep. You're even in a rut with the ties you wear. What do you have, three in your closet that you alternate on some kind of fixed schedule?"

Bruce lifted his chin. "I own seven ties, one for each day of the week. And I happen to like my gray pinstriped suit. It's important I look the part if my clients are to have confidence in my counseling. I learned that from my father."

"I've never met your father, Bruce. Does he wear pinstriped suits, too?"

"That's the only kind of suit he's ever worn, and you cannot deny that he built up a highly successful clientele of celebrities over the years. Nor can you deny that I've done well following in his footsteps."

Arline pulled a shirt from the rack and examined it more closely. "I'm sure you're a highly qualified psychologist," she replied. "And I have my suspicions it was your money that attracted Jenice to you in the first place. But if you want to get her into a wedding dress, you're going to have to realize she's more than one of your clients. She's a woman who craves excitement and adventure in her life, Bruce. And a steady diet of your kind of wardrobe is anything but exciting. Here," she said, handing him the shirt she had picked to go with the tan slacks. "Go try these on. In the meantime, I'll see if I can find you a blue blazer and a couple of outfits to match."

"I know you're only trying to help, Arline," Bruce grumped. "But I hate being treated like a child."

"Have we come full circle, or what?" Jason laughed. "I remember when Sam hated Bruce treating her like a child, and now you're doing it to him, Arline. I may end up enjoying this assignment more than I thought."

"What do you find so amusing?" Bruce asked, as Arline suddenly giggled for no apparent reason.

"Never mind, Bruce," she said with a wink toward Jason. "Just go try on the outfit."

Muttering something inaudible under his breath, Bruce headed for the dressing rooms with the clothing over his arm.

"I've got to hand it to you, Arline," Jason said, as he gleefully watched Bruce walk away. "You sure knew where to find the starting line for this Mission Impossible project. But do you really think putting the wimp in some decent clothes will make him anything more than a well-dressed wimp?"

"Stop calling him a wimp, Jason," Arline spoke distractedly. "And see if you can find some suitable ties while I look at the sport coats."

"Why not put him in a George Strait hat and pair of leather boots? Maybe we could even get him some guitar lessons. No, come to think of it, that won't work. There aren't enough songs with the word 'darling' in them."

"Jason Hackett!" Arline snapped. "This is your project we're working on. Now find me some decent ties and stop with the stand-up comic routine, okay?"

It took the rest of the day and seven men's clothing stores, but before she was finished Arline had maneuvered Bruce into purchasing an entire new wardrobe. The only item she was a little concerned about was the "Home Improvement" tie with the electrical outlet on it that Jason had insisted upon. It did add a certain casual look, though, so long as Bruce was careful where he wore it.

"I hope you know what you're doing," Bruce mutttered as he

loaded the last of his purchases in the back of his Lexus. "I really feel conspicuous in Levi's Dockers and a polo shirt. I trust you're not planning on having me go where I might run into someone I know."

"I hadn't thought about it until you brought it up, Bruce. But I think that's an excellent idea for our next move. What was the name of that restaurant, Jason? You know, the one where you observed Bruce and Jenice together?"

Jason chuckled. "You know what, Arline?" he asked. "You have a mean streak a mile wide. I like the way you think. The restaurant is the Hunter's Cottage, over on Rose Boulevard."

"To the Hunter's Cottage," Arline said, with a commanding wave in the general direction of the place. "I'm starved, and whatever they serve there sounds like what I'm in the mood for right now."

Bruce flipped on his turn signal and pulled into the left lane at the next light. "I'm beginning to remember why I dislike that pesky ghost so intensely. I suppose he's having a good laugh at my expense right now."

"Oh, no, Bruce. To the contrary, he just remarked how nice you look in your new outfit. He thinks the idea of letting some of your friends see you dressed like this will be good for your new image."

"I what?!" Jason choked.

"He said what?" Bruce echoed.

"Okay, so I stretched his reaction a bit. What's the big deal? Here's our plan. After an early dinner, we drop the things we bought off at your place. Then it's time for you to start contributing something toward the project. I want you to come up with a fun place to take me out for a date. I realize I'm not Jenice, but I'll just have to do until you get the hang of this having fun thing. And no, you can't change back into your old clothes before you take me on the date."

"But, Arline, I feel so conspicuous wearing these clothes."

"You'll get over it. In fact, I plan on coming over to your place sometime next week to check out your closet. Anything I find in there that I don't like is gone. I'll give you the choice on how to dispose of the stuff, but I suggest you consider donating them to a needy charity. Personally, I'd rather burn them, but—"

The light turned green and Bruce set the car in motion with an abrupt jerk. "I don't want to give my clothes away," he protested. "If you insist on my wearing these new things, at least let me put my comfortable clothes away somewhere. There's always the chance Jenice will turn me down, and I may need them later."

"No way!" came Arline's curt reply. "I'm not investing my time in improving your character only to have you slide back into your dungeon of gloom if you fail to find your pot of gold at the end of this rainbow. The clothes go, and that's final. Now get your mind on more important things and come up with a place to take me on a date tonight."

"How about taking in a play?"

"Nope, too dull. Think of something else."

"We could make it a comedy. Laughter is never dull, and you know what they say about it being good for the soul."

"Ask him if he'd like to take you on the roller-coaster he once rode with Sam and me," Jason suggested in amusement from the backseat.

"You rode a roller-coaster?" Arline asked in surprise.

"Roller-coaster? What on earth are you talking about, Arline?"

"Jason said you once rode a roller-coaster with him and Sam. He suggested you take me there tonight."

"No! Please! Give me a chance. I'll think of something else, I promise. But don't make me get back on that roller coaster. I was sick for a week the last time."

Arline laughed so hard it hurt. "All right, Bruce," she conceded. "No roller coaster. But you'd better come up with something more exciting than *The Phantom of the Opera* or I'm liable to change my mind."

As Bruce brought the Lexus to a stop in front of the Hunter's Cottage, Arline caught sight of a racy red and blue motorcycle parked near the entrance to the building.

"Wow!" she cried. "Would you look at that. I wouldn't turn down a date with you if you picked me up on something like that, Bruce."

Bruce sniffed. "The motorcycle belongs to Ted Freeman, the parking valet here at the restaurant. It's his pride and joy. The management allows him to park it where he can keep an eye on it. He tells me it's what he refers to as a 'high pilferage item. That means—"

"I know what it means, Bruce. You don't need to draw me a picture."

In three bounds, Ted was around the car and instantly had Arline's door open. Once she was out, he scampered to the opposite side and opened Bruce's door. "Don't mind me," Jason chuckled, as Arline looked on in amusement, "I'll just step through my own door."

"I really like your motorcycle," Arline said, just as Ted was about to get in the car. "What is it?"

Ted's face lit up like a room full of candles at her question. "It's a Kawasaki KLX 650," He proudly answered. "Are you into bikes, ma'am?"

"No, not really. But I'd like to go for a ride on this one sometime. It looks like it would be fun."

"Say, your voice sounds familiar. You're not Arline Wilson, by chance?"

"Yes," she beamed. "I'm Arline. Have you heard my show?"

"I listen almost every day. By the way, who was that guy they had filling in for you today?"

"I'm not sure who did the show today, Ted. I'm on—well, let's just call it a vacation."

"You called me Ted! All right! Arline Wilson knows me by name. Say, I really liked the angel thing you came up with. How did you ever think that up, anyway?"

"Oh, it was easy, Ted. I just met an angel, that's all. He's here right now if you'd like to say hello to him."

"Where?" Ted laughed, getting into the swing of the conversation.

"Right here," Arline answered, pointing to Jason. "Ted, this is Jason. Jason, this is Ted."

"Are you having fun, Arline?" Jason asked sarcastically.

"Hi ya, Jason," Ted said, smiling like a child just handed an ice cream cone. "Would you like your cloud parked or anything?"

Jason couldn't help himself, he broke out laughing. "You're all right, Ted," he replied. "If I owned a cloud, I'd let you be the one to park it every time."

"I used to ride a Honda 90 when I was a youngster," Bruce said, trying to enter the conversation. "It belonged to my cousin. She rode up hills and everything. I just kept it on the pavement, but I once had it up to forty-five miles an hour."

"I'm impressed," Ted answered, sliding behind the wheel of the Lexus and pulling the door closed behind him. "And I like your new outfit, too. I've never seen you in anything alive before, Bruce. It does things for you, man."

"Thank you," Bruce replied halfheartedly.

"Come by my place sometime, Bruce. I'll let you and Arline use a couple of my other bikes to go for a spin in the hills behind my house. Sorry, though. My Kawasaki's off-limits."

"Thanks, Ted, but—" Bruce began.

"We'll do that, Ted," Arline said, cutting Bruce off in midsentence. Ted gave her a thumbs-up and drove off toward the parking lot.

"I hadn't thought about you, Jason," Arline said as she and Bruce were being shown to their table for dinner. "I mean, there's no way you can order a meal in this place, is there?"

"Let me guess," Bruce whispered, making sure no one but Arline could hear. "This mysterious fellow you called Gus is bringing the ghost a Big Mac or something. I remember how it was when I was dating Samantha."

Jason laughed. "Not this time, Bruce. Gus is off in some distant part of the universe right now. Anyway, Arline, don't worry about me. I just happen to be the head chef in a place that puts this one to shame. If I wanted to, I could bring something in from there. But to tell you the truth, I'd rather just wander through the kitchen while the two of you eat. Being invisible, I can pick up on any of their secrets I might be interested in."

"Enjoy yourself then," Arline said as she slid into the chair Bruce was holding for her. "I'll see you when you tire of your little game."

Ted was not the only one to notice the change in Bruce's appearance. There were remarks from the hostess and three waiters. The organist even dedicated a song to him: "It's Time for a Cool Change." Everyone in the place enjoyed it, except Bruce, who scowled throughout the entire meal.

Just as the waiter returned with the check, Arline happened to glance at a nearby table, where she saw something that struck her as unusual. Jason was there, kneeling next to a French poodle that was tied to a leash at the table of an older couple. Arline was certain the animal was responding to Jason's attention.

I'll ask him about that later, she told herself.

"Well," she said, turning her attention back to Bruce, "have you thought of an exciting place to take me on our date tonight?" She folded her napkin and laid it next to her empty plate.

Bruce wiped the corner of his mouth and dropped his own napkin to the table. "I'm sure you know how difficult this is for me, Arline. Much as I hate to admit it, I'm just not an exciting person. I have given it some thought, however, and I've come up with a suggestion. I have a friend in the motion picture business, Howard Placard, who owns a private beach. Samantha had me rent a red Mustang convertible and take her there once. It's a little late to rent a convertible this evening, but we could go for a moonlight walk on the beach."

Arline thought about it for a moment or two. "Is that the same beach where Jenice wants you to drop from the sky and propose to her, by any chance?"

"Yes, it's the same beach. The two of us were there a couple of times, too. Always at her suggestion, of course."

"Okay," Arline agreed. "An evening on the beach will do for starters. It's a little too cool to do any swimming this early in the year, but I have an idea that will be just as much fun. And by the way, I like the idea of the convertible, too. How about if you cancel your appointments again tomorrow, and we trade your Lexus in on one?"

Bruce choked. "Don't you think that's going a little far? I mean, my Lexus is the image I need. A Mustang convertible is nothing more than a grown man's toy."

"Either you agree to trading cars, or I'm going to stand up and shout to everyone in this place that you just proposed to me. I'll even get the organist to play the wedding march."

"You wouldn't do that!"

Arline smiled. "Oh, yeah? Just watch me."

"No!" Bruce cried out reaching across the table to keep Arline from standing. "I'll buy a convertible tomorrow. But can I at least keep my Lexus, too?"

"I don't know. You might be tempted to backslide if the Lexus is handy."

"I'll leave it parked up the mountain in my parents' garage, all right?"

"Only if you let me hold on to the keys. Now, do I make the announcement, or do we have a deal?"

"We have a deal," Bruce sighed. "But only if you promise never to ask me to sell my house."

On the way to the beach, Arline had Bruce stop at a K-Mart, where she asked him wait while she ran into the store. When she returned to the car, she had a large package that she placed in the backseat.

"What is it?" Bruce asked.

"You'll find out later," Arline laughed. "I told you I had an idea to take the place of swimming."

"Is the ghost still with us?" Bruce asked, once they were back on the road.

"He's in the back, and that reminds me," she said, turning to face Jason. "I saw you talking to a French poodle back at the restaurant. Did the dog actually know you were there?"

"Yeah," Jason answered. "It's the darnedest thing, but some animals can see me, while others can't. It's something I learned while I was hanging around waiting for the chance to reveal myself to Sam. I've been meaning to ask someone on the other side how that works, but it keeps slipping my mind."

"How about that?" Arline turned back to Bruce. "Jason tells me animals can sometimes see him. Don't you find that interesting?"

Bruce gave her a pained look. "Is it really necessary for him to be with us everywhere we go? I can't help feeling uncomfortable, knowing he's around."

"You're not really giving him a fair chance, Bruce," Arline scolded him. "Jason's a great guy, and you have to admit it's not your everyday adventure having an angel keeping you company."

"I'm sorry, Arline, but there are some things I'll never be able to change about myself. It's true, I've been forced into believing the ghost is real, but learning to like him is another matter altogether."

"Ah," Jason groaned. "That breaks my heart, wimp. Especially since I've tried so hard to befriend you and all."

By the time they arrived at the private beach, a nearly full moon shone brightly in the sky over the calm water. There was just enough breeze to gently ruffle Arline's shoulder-length reddish-brown hair.

"This is perfect," she said, pulling the package from the backseat and handing it to Bruce.

"A kite?" Bruce asked, looking into the sack. "What do you want me to do with a kite, Arline?"

"What a dumb question, Bruce. Put it together, of course. How can we fly it if you don't put it together? You can put a kite together, can't you?"

"I—I've never assembled a kite before," he said, staring at the yellow paper rolled tightly around two sticks.

"What?" Arline asked in surprise. "Don't tell me you let your father build all your kites for you."

"You don't understand, Arline. I've never flown a kite before. When I was a child, I asked my father to buy me one once and teach me to use it, but he never got around to it."

A lump formed in Arline's throat. "Your father never flew a kite with you?" she managed to ask. "What kind of games did he play with you?"

Bruce thought for a moment. "Well, he took me to see a baseball game once. In fact, that game is one of my happiest memories. When I was a young boy I used to lay awake nights reliving the game over and over again. It's been years since I've thought about it, but even now it brings back pleasant feelings."

Arline stared at Bruce. Suddenly, she was seeing him in a way she never had before. Her heart ached as she visualized his childhood and understood for the first time what made Bruce the way he was now.

As she realized the depth of the problem she faced, the magnitude of changing his personality loomed greater than ever. With that realization, however, came an even more burning desire to succeed in her goal. No longer was her friendship with Samantha the driving force behind teaching Bruce how to live a richer life. Now her motive was raised to a more personal level. Taking the kite from him, she began unrolling the paper.

"Here, Bruce," she said, without a trace of condescension in her voice. "I'll help you put it together."

It took nearly ten minutes, but with Arline talking him through it, Bruce managed to get the kite assembled. "I did it!" he shouted, smiling like a boy on Christmas morning. "I put the kite together."

"Yes, you certainly did" Arline laughed. "Now, let's see if you can get it to fly."

Not giving up after two futile attempts, Bruce pulled off his shoes and stood with the cool ocean breeze to his face. With a deep breath, he broke into a run, letting out the string a little at a time. As Arline watched the kite settle onto the wind and begin its steep ascent into the evening sky, she leaped into the air, wildly clapping her hands.

"You did it!" she squealed as Bruce came to a stop and fed more line to the ever-climbing kite.

"Yeah, he did," Jason shouted back. "Darned if I'm not proud of the wimp myself."

For the next two hours Bruce and Arline sat side by side on a large flat rock, enjoying the sounds and smell of the ocean and flying their kite in the soft light of the moon. For the most part, Bruce remained in quiet thought and Arline knew it was Jenice who was on his mind. For some odd reason she couldn't possibly explain, she felt a twinge of jealousy.

CHAPTER TEN

Saturday morning found Arline awake much earlier than usual. Although she normally loved to sleep late, there was just too much to think about. On top of being visited by an angel and facing the prospect of a great new job, she was now confronted with thoughts of Bruce that refused to leave her alone. Crazy as the notion seemed, she was beginning to enjoy helping him with his problem.

What's the matter with you, Arline Wilson, she asked herself after tossing off the covers and sitting up on the edge of the bed. *This is the same Bruce Vincent you've known for more than two years. Why are you looking at him so differently now? All you're expected to do is teach him how to put a little fun and excitement into his listless life. You don't have to worry about what made him the way he is. More important, you don't have to get personally involved with him. After all, you have enough to think about with your wonderful new job starting in just a few weeks. So let's not get our priorities out of order here. Just do the job Jason's asking of you, and let it go at that.*

After a quick shower, Arline slipped on a pair of blue jeans and a white western-style blouse. She heard Jason singing to himself in the kitchen, and she smiled. "Did you stick this close to Sam when you were haunting her?" she asked, entering the room. "Or do you think I enjoy finding an uninvited man in my house first thing in the morning?"

"I wasn't haunting her, and you didn't say a word to me about not inviting myself in. With Sam it was different. She had dozens of rules I had to follow. One of them kept me from ever entering her apartment without asking permission first. She wasn't as willing to have me around as you seem to be, Arline. Not at first, anyway."

"That's because you're staying close to me for a different reason. You need my help. And the help you gave me pulling down a great new job doesn't hurt your image, either. In Sam's case, you popped in one day exclaiming you were in love with her. I can see where that would make a big difference in the way you were accepted. At least in the beginning. After she fell in love with you, I'm sure she didn't mind having you around. Although, I can imagine how hard it must have been for her dating an angel."

"You got that right. We had our problems, but we enjoyed being with each other in spite of them all. Neither of us knew how it would all turn out in the end, but we had Gus's proposition of getting me a new body to cling to."

Arline sighed. "I only wish I had known then what I know now," she sighed. "I could have been some help to Sam when she came to me with the story of a ghost in her life. As it was, I can't help feeling I let her down. She needed someone to talk to, and I only turned her off."

Jason protested. "That's not true, Arline. Sam told me about the conversation the two of you had about me. She said your willingness to accept her friendship, with no questions of what she meant by being in love with a ghost, was a tremendous boost at a time she needed it the most."

Arline looked at Jason hopefully. "Did she really say that, Jason?"

"She did."

"I miss her, you know," she said sadly. "She was like my sister."

"She misses you, too, Arline. But take my word for it, the two of you will be friends again when the time comes. I'm in a better position to understand that than you are, and I give you my word, it's all true."

"You probably are in a better position to know those things," Arline laughed.

"You know, Arline," Jason said humbly. "I misjudged the way you approached Bruce with what the two of us are up to. I thought you had blown it for sure when you told him about me. I was wrong. It's obvious you have everything under control. I have to admit, you really know how to handle the wimp."

Arline couldn't help but laugh at Jason's comment about Bruce. "First off," she replied, "I wish you'd stop calling him a wimp. After that, Mr. Angel, I suggest you hang onto your halo, because what you saw yesterday was only the beginning. By the time the fifteenth of April rolls around, I'll have Bruce ready to jump from that airplane with his hands tied behind his back."

Jason's eyes widened in shock. "You're absolutely sure of that, Arline? Do you have any idea how many things have gone wrong on April fifteenth over the years?"

"I know it's the day income tax comes due every year," she answered. "Is there more?"

"Yeah, as a matter of fact there is. Abe Lincoln died on that day in 1865, and in 1912 the Titanic sank in the cold waters of the North Atlantic."

"How do you know?" Arline asked, her disbelief evident in her voice.

"Maggie told me when I stopped by the office on my way to your place this morning."

Arline gasped as the realization shook her. "I'd say it might be better never to mention this to Bruce. Don't you agree?"

"I couldn't agree more. Even *you* couldn't get him out of that airplane if he knew about those things."

"Never mind," Arline said bravely. "By the time he's ready to make that parachute jump, I'll have him in shape. He'll be braver than the Lone Ranger, happier than the Cheshire Cat, and more fun loving than a whole forest full of Robin Hoods. You have my word on that."

* * *

"If you'll sign right here, Mr. Vincent, you'll be the proud owner of a fully loaded red Mustang convertible." The saleswoman at Vermont Ford handed Bruce a pen. After one last glance at Arline, whose smile told him he had better not back out now, Bruce signed the paper.

It was Arline who ran the top down and drove the Mustang off the lot. Bruce was in the Lexus, leading the two-car caravan up the scenic drive to his parents' mountain home.

"I have to give it to the old boy," Jason said to Arline as they drove. "He's taking the loss of his beloved Lexus pretty well. That guy must make the bucks, though. I've never seen anyone pay cash for a new car before. I don't get it, either. Most psychologists I've known of in the past didn't make that kind of money."

Arline drew in a deep breath of clean mountain air and leaned against the back of the seat allowing her hair to blow freely in the wind. It felt good.

"That's because most psychologists don't have the same clients as Bruce," she replied. "He caters to the famous and wealthy. His father established the clientele long before Bruce got in the business, and it just continues to get better as the years go by. Bruce may be what you like to refer to as a wimp, but he's good at his profession. He never loses a client, and they all refer their friends to him."

Jason shuddered. "Yeah, I hate to think how close I came to losing Sam to Bruce and all his money."

Arline gave Jason a dirty look. "What's the matter with you, Jason? You know Sam would never have married Bruce just for his money. There had to be something in the man that attracted her to him."

"I suppose so," Jason conceded reluctantly, "but I'll never understand what it was till the day I die. Uh . . . just kidding about the day I die, Arline," he said as she turned to glare at him.

Arline shook her head and looked back at the road ahead. "With a sick sense of humor like yours, I sometimes wonder what Sam sees in you."

"Ouch! That smarts."

"Hey, come off it," she laughed. "I'm only exhibiting some of my own sick humor with that remark. You're exactly the kind Sam would go for. I have no trouble at all putting the two of you together. And that comes from the best friend Sam ever had. I knew and loved her more than I could have loved my own sister, if I'd had one."

"Why do you keep using the past tense, Arline? I've told you that Sam is just on the other side of a rainbow from you. She's still the Sam you know and love, and the two of you are still best friends. Knowing what I know now, I can promise that in what seems like no time at all you'll find yourself shopping with Sam again. Only this time it will be in a mall so fabulous there are no words in this dimension to describe it."

Arline said quietly, "You give me goose bumps talking like that, Jason. I believe you're telling the truth, but it all seems so far away right now it's hard to imagine."

"Tell me something, Arline," Jason asked, returning to the former subject. "You're a beautiful, young, single woman. What do you think it was Sam saw in Bruce?"

"You think I'm beautiful?" she asked with a blush moving quickly up her face.

"Are you kidding? You could be a model if you wanted to."

"Thanks, Jason. You really know how to make a woman's day. To answer your question about Bruce, he is a kind, gentle, and generous man. I have no doubt he loved Sam very much, as I'm sure he loves Jenice now. He has no bad habits that I know of. He even gave up his occasional glass of wine while he was still going with Sam. He knew how she disliked him drinking wine, and he wanted to please her. I know how abrasive he can be, but he can also be romantic and tender. I'm only now beginning to see some of the possibilities that Sam must have seen in him long ago. I'm not sure this answers your question, Jason, but it's as close as I can come to it."

"Thanks, Arline. Much as it hurts to admit, I may have misjudged the old boy. I'll give him this much, he's trying hard to come around. Although he still has a long way to go."

Arline watched as Bruce turned the Lexus off the main road onto a long horseshoe drive. She followed behind him.

"Wow!" she said as the Vincents' home came into view. "Would you look at that. Bruce told me his parents lived in a nice place, but I never pictured anything like this."

"Tell me about it," Jason chuckled. "Sam loved this house so much, she talked Gus into getting us one similar to it on the other side. Ours has some conveniences that aren't available in this one, but the layout is pretty much the same, mountains and all."

"Sam and her mountains," Arline reminisced. "It doesn't surprise me she would have chosen a place like this one, if given the chance."

"Given the chance?" Jason laughed. "She didn't wait to be given the chance. She backed Gus into a corner until he had no choice but to include the house in the contract. The poor guy didn't know what hit him."

"That's the Sam I knew . . . uh . . . know," Arline grinned, as she pulled alongside Bruce's car and shut off the engine. Even before she had time to unbuckle her seatbelt, Bruce had her door open. "Are you positive you won't change your mind about me leaving my Lexus here?" he pleaded. "I love this car, Arline."

"What do you love the most?" Arline came back. "Your Lexus or Jenice?"

Bruce answered with a long sigh, then taking Arline by the arm, he led the way to the front door. On the porch, he stared at the doorbell switch. "No," he said. "Not this time I won't."

"You won't what?" Arline asked.

"I won't ring the doorbell. I'm just going to walk in like I owned the place."

Arline didn't understand his hesitance. "It's your parents' home, Bruce. You should be able to walk in without ringing the doorbell."

"That may be true, but it's something I've never done before." Throwing out his chest, Bruce twisted the knob and pushed open the door. "Hello, Mother," he called out. "Are you home?"

Arline had never met either of Bruce's parents, though she remembered Samantha speaking highly of them. It didn't take long for them to win Arline over as well. After introductions all around, they sat down to a scrumptious lunch of homemade bread and split pea soup. Not once did Bruce's parents say anything to make Arline feel uncomfortable, although she knew they must wonder why she was with him instead of Jenice. The conversation stayed mainly on the change in Bruce's appearance and of his decision to buy a convertible. Ruth Vincent was happy and even excited about both prospects. On the other hand, Bruce's father was a little cool over the changes in his son.

Throughout lunch, Arline studied Bruce's parents closely. Ruth reminded her of an elegant movie actress whose beauty and charm in her younger years had grown even more radiant with time. It was easy to understand why Samantha had loved her so. Turning her attention to Bruce's father, Arline couldn't help wonder what had caused him to be the "arm's length" kind of father that Bruce had described. His resemblance to Bruce was uncanny, and she had to laugh inwardly when she saw he was wearing the same sort of drab clothes Bruce had always favored. Then an idea struck her.

Maybe it's never too late for a father and son to learn how to bond with each other, she thought.

It was not until lunch was finished and everything cleaned up that she made her move. When she did, it began with a question to Bruce's father.

"So tell me, Kent," she asked, as the group retired to the living room, "are there any lakes around here where the fishing's good?"

Kent looked at Arline with one eye squinted. "Yes," he answered cautiously, after only a moment's thought. "There's Lake Sundown about five miles up the road. I've heard the fishing is good there, though I've never been one to indulge in the sport myself."

"You're not a fisherman?" Arline asked, trying to sound surprised. "I don't believe this. Here you are, retired in a place that most fisherman only dream of, and you're not a fisherman yourself. You know what? I'll bet if you tried it once, you'd learn to love it. What do you say we all drive up to the lake where you and Bruce can rent a boat and give it a try? Ruth and I can fish from the bank and get a little better acquainted."

Bruce's father coughed. "I . . . uh . . . don't know, Arline." It was obvious that he didn't know how to respond to her suggestion.

Arline glanced over at Ruth to see her reaction. As their eyes met, a strange thing happened. It was as if their minds linked together without saying a word. Arline knew exactly what Ruth was thinking, and she knew Ruth was on to her little game, as well.

"I think it's a wonderful idea," Ruth said with a wink. "Only it might be better for the three of you to go without me. I need to prepare a presentation for a women's conference tomorrow, and I could use the time alone. It would also give Kent and Bruce a chance to spend some time together without me along. I think it would be good for both of them, don't you, Arline?"

Arline gave a wink in return. "I do think it would be nice for them both," she agreed.

"But Ruth, darling," Kent protested. "I don't even own a fishing rod."

"You can rent everything you need at the store by the lake," Ruth was quick to remind him. "What do you think, Bruce? Would you like to try your hand at fishing with Arline and your father?"

"Well, Mother, I . . . ."

Half an hour later the four of them—if you count Jason, that is—loaded into a rowboat with enough fishing tackle and bait to fully equip the two reluctant men. Arline declined a pole of her own, saying she would help Bruce with his. After five minutes or so of rowing in circles, Bruce got the hang of the oars and managed a course for the center of the lake.

"I've scoped the place out," Jason said once they were under way. "There's a large school of trout feeding near the shore under the shade of that big pine tree over there." He pointed in the direction of the tree he was referring to.

"You mean you can see underwater, too?" Arline whispered. Fortunately, there was just enough breeze blowing that the sound of rustling tree branches along the shores of the lake covered her voice. No one but Jason heard.

"Hey," Jason answered, with a proud shrug. "I have the best built-in scuba equipment you can imagine. Not only can I see perfectly below the surface of the water, but I don't even have to come up for air."

Arline was curious enough that she would like to have quizzed Jason further on the subject, but this was not a good time. Instead, she said to Bruce, "Why don't you pull the boat over next to the bank under the shade of that tree. It looks like the perfect place to me."

Bruce didn't argue, and he soon had the boat anchored in exactly the right spot. "What do we do now?" he asked, picking up the rented pole and staring at it as if it were a strange object from another planet. "I've never used one of these in my life."

"You bait your hook," Arline smiled, handing Bruce the carton of worms.

"You expect me to put one of those things on this little hook?"

"Oh, brother," Jason laughed. "This guy's an even bigger wimp than I gave him credit for."

"We came out here so you could catch a fish," Arline persisted. "And you can't do that without bait. How hard can it be for a man your size to put something so small as a worm on the hook? So far as I know, there's never been a recorded case where someone died from a worm bite."

Bruce gazed at the carton in his hand. "Couldn't we just enjoy ourselves by rowing around the lake a bit, instead of fishing?" Arline didn't have to answer his question. The glare in her eyes told Bruce he'd better not push his luck further. With a grimace bigger than the month of October, he put a finger into the moist soil and pulled out a long, fat, wiggly worm. There he paused, as if by waiting long enough this whole unpleasant business of fishing would somehow go away.

"The worm's not going to crawl onto your hook by itself, Bruce," Arline said sternly. "You're going to have put it there. And just remember this, if you can't force yourself to do something so simple as baiting a hook, how are you ever going to talk yourself into parachuting out of a perfectly good airplane?"

Kent looked at Bruce. "Did she say you were going to parachute from an airplane?" he asked. "Why would you want to do something as reckless as that, son?"

"It's a long story, Father. I'll explain it to you later." Then, with Arline and Kent looking on, Bruce moved a trembling handful of worm toward the hook. It took a while, but he managed to get the job done.

Smiling like a Boy Scout who had just successfully started his first campfire without a match, Bruce glanced up at his father.

"Don't look at me, son," his father stammered. "I'll just help you get your fish into the boat instead of fishing myself."

"No wonder Bruce is such a wimp," Jason snorted. "He had a father who trained him to be one. They say the acorn never falls far from the tree. Looking at these two, I'd have to agree with that analogy. Okay. Tell the old boy to set his bobber at about three feet and drop his line in exactly here." Jason pointed to a spot not far from the boat on the side nearest the shore. "And get ready for some fun, because I'm going to help him catch the grandaddy of the lake. You can't believe the size of this fellow, and he's just lying there waiting for his dinner to come to him."

Arline smiled and winked at Jason. "Here, let me help you set your bobber," she said, adjusting it to the point Jason had suggested. "Now, ease your line into the water right about here."

Bruce's lack of interest couldn't have been more noticeable if he were holding a sign declaring it. Slowly, he extended the line over the water and allowed it to settle down where Arline had pointed. The bobber came to rest, white side up, where it moved lazily up and down with the motion of the water.

"What am I supposed to do next?" Bruce grumbled. Arline looked toward Jason for his next instruction.

"Everything looks great. The bait is only inches from the nose of the big guy, but he's a lazy one. Have Bruce jiggle the line up and down a bit to add a little challenge to the game."

"Wiggle your line a little bit," Arline said, passing on the instruction. Bruce jerked his line.

"Not that much," Jason snapped. "Just a gentle movement to attract the fish's interest."

Arline nodded her understanding. "Slow down a little, Bruce. Just move your line up and down gently to make your bait more appealing to a hungry fish." Bruce exhaled loudly in disgust but did as Arline asked.

"Get ready for the fun," Jason exclaimed. "Here it comes!"

It all happened so quickly, Arline felt as if she were watching one of those silent movies where everything is speeded up. The little bobber vanished below the surface of the black water to the screaming whir of nylon line flying off the face of Bruce's reel. Bruce gripped the rod and stared wide-eyed at the water.

"What do I do now?" he shouted desperately.

Arline shot forward. Throwing an arm around Bruce, she forced his thumb against the tension lever and watched as the end of the pole bent until it nearly touched the water. Placing her other hand under his, she guided him through the motion of raising the pole to keep the line from going slack while playing the fish.

"You're doing fine, Bruce," she said calmly. "Just let him have some line, but keep enough pressure on to make him work for every inch he takes."

She felt Bruce's already tight muscles tense even further as the big fish broke water and shot nearly two feet upward while fighting violently to free himself from the firmly set hook. The sound of five pounds of struggling trout crashing back to the lake's surface was lost completely behind the piercing scream Bruce sent echoing to every ear within half a mile.

"Relax, Bruce," Arline whispered soothingly. "Let him play just a bit longer. Then you can begin reeling him in." Twice more the big fish broke water before Arline moved Bruce's hand to the lever and helped him slowly take up the line.

In all, it was more than ten minutes before Kent, following Arline's instructions, netted the exhausted trout and pulled him into the boat. For a long moment Bruce and Arline remained close together, Arline's arms cradled around his shoulders. A feeling of almost frightening warmth filled Arline's whole body, and she quickly pulled away, moving to the far end of the boat.

"You did it, son!" Kent shouted. "You caught the biggest fish I've ever seen in my life."

"I did, didn't I?" Bruce responded, never taking his eyes off Arline.

"You know, I had just a little bit to do with this," Jason said, showing a hint jealousy in his voice.

"Of course you did, Jason," Arline said, forgetting to lower her voice.

Kent looked puzzled. "Who are you talking to, Arline? There's no Jason here, unless you've decided to give a name to the fish."

Arline couldn't believe what happened next. Before she could think up an excuse for her slip of the tongue, Bruce jumped into the conversation with a stunning and completely unexpected declaration. "She's talking to Jason Hackett, Father," he volunteered. "Jason is a ghost who likes to go around haunting beautiful women."

"A ghost?" Kent's father laughed loudly. "Well now, that's a first. I've never heard you try to make jokes before, Bruce. What brought this on, anyway?"

"It's no joke, Father. Jason is not only real, but he's right here with us at this very moment. In fact, I suspect he had a lot to do with my catching that fish."

"I sincerely hope you're attempting to make a joke," Kent grumbled. "Because if you're not, you've lost your mind."

"Believe me, Father, I know perfectly well how hard this is for you to understand. I'm a psychologist, too. Accepting the reality of the ghost was one of the most difficult things I've ever done. But I assure you, he is real. I'll prove it to you if you have any change in your pocket. Do you?"

"Certainly I have change in my pocket."

"Take the change from your pocket and hold it out behind you over the lake. Arline will have the ghost tell you how much money is in your hand."

"Arline will tell you? If you see a ghost in the boat with us, why would you need Arline to tell you what he might say?"

"I can neither see nor hear the ghost, Father. Arline is the only one here who can do that. Please do as I ask. Hold out the change in your pocket."

"This is preposterous," Kent huffed. "I'll do no such thing."

"Father! You're being stubborn. How else can I prove to you that Jason is really here with us if you refuse to participate in my little experiment?"

Kent fixed his eyes on his son with a look of contempt. Reluctantly, he reached into his trouser pocket and removed everything he had in there. Following Bruce's direction, he held it all out over the lake.

Jason laughed. "I should leave him hanging," he snickered. "Wouldn't it be great fun watching him try and explain his way out of this one?"

"Jason Hackett!" Arline scolded. "Don't you even think of pulling a stunt like that. You tell me what Kent has in his hand this instant!"

"You remind me of Sam when you're angry, Arline," Jason teased.

"Jason!"

"All right, all right. He's holding thirty-five cents, a fingernail clipper, and a brown button with four thread holes in it."

"You have thirty-five cents in change," Arline repeated. "Along with a fingernail clipper and brown button with four holes in it."

"What is this?" Kent demanded loudly. "What are the two of you up to?"

"What we're up to," Bruce explained bluntly, "is proving to you that Jason Hackett is not only a ghost, but that he's here with us at this very minute. I have to say, Father, this is the first time I can remember ever seeing you at a loss for words."

"Well, of course I'm at a loss for words, Bruce. Your little joke is making me very angry."

Bruce looked at his father in amazement. "You're more than angry. You're really quite flustered. You know, this is the first time I've ever enjoyed having this ghost around. And you know what? I've just thought of something that can make having him around even more fun. I'm going to ask him to tell me what's in that chest you've kept hidden away all these years."

"Oh," Kent said, cramming the items back into his pocket. "So that's what this is all about. You think you can trick me into telling you the best-kept secret of my life? Ha! I've never even told your mother what's in that chest. It's my business alone, and it will remain my business until the day I die. And just for your information, I've stipulated in my will to have the box destroyed without ever opening it."

"Jason," Bruce said, with a grin spreading across his face, "I know you can hear me. I've never asked anything of you before, but I'd really like to ask you a special favor now. In my father's study, there's a large oak chest with a brass padlock securing it closed. I must have asked my father a thousand times what it is he keeps in that chest, but he always refuses to tell me. I've never been so curious about anything in my life. I know you and I haven't exactly been the best of friends, Jason, and I wouldn't blame you for turning me down. But if you can find it in your heart to help me out here, I'll be forever in your debt."

Arline smiled at the thought of Bruce asking Jason for a favor. "Can you do it?" she asked. "I mean, it's bound to be pretty dark inside an old chest. Can you see what's in there?"

"It's useless, Arline," Kent said smugly. "I'll never reveal what's in my trunk. You might as well give up this silly little game right now."

"Oh, no," Bruce remembered. "I forgot that Jason can't see in the dark. When Samantha first tried to tell me about him, I wrote something on a business card and tossed it into the backseat of my Lexus. It was after dark, though, and I had to turn the light on for him to read what I had written on the card."

Jason broke out laughing. "Tell the wimp I was only having some fun at his expense that night. Seeing in the dark happens to be a very simple matter for an experienced angel like me. And I will do what he asks, too. On one condition, that is."

"What condition?" Arline asked.

"I want Bruce to stop calling me a ghost. I hate being called a ghost. I'll check out the chest for him, if he'll give me his word never to call me a ghost again."

Okay," Arline said, after thoughtfully considering Jason's request. "I'll approach him with your offer on one condition of my own. If he stops calling you a ghost, you have to agree to stop calling him a wimp."

"What are the two of you talking about?" Bruce asked dejectedly. "I told you, I already know he can't do what I asked."

"Yes, he can, Bruce. He was just giving you a hard time about turning on the car light. Now, give it a second, will you? I'm in the middle of a negotiation here. What do you say, Jason? Is it a deal?"

"Even if I don't call him a wimp, I'll be thinking it," Jason grumbled. "What's the difference?"

"The difference is I won't have to listen to it," Arline snapped. "You're forgetting I'm only here as a favor to you in the first place. Having the two of you constantly at each other's jugular isn't my idea of a good time."

"I guess you're right, Arline," Jason said. "I should have a little more respect for your feelings. If calling Bruce a wimp really bothers you, I'll give it a rest."

Arline's tone was definite. "It really bothers me."

"Okay, I'll trust you to convince Bruce on the ghost thing while I'm checking out his father's chest."

"Do you have any idea how hard it is, being in on only one side of a conversation like this?" Bruce complained. "Will you please tell me what's going on?"

"Jason agreed, Bruce. He's on his way to your father's study now. He has put one condition on doing this favor for you, though. He has this hang-up about being called a ghost, and he wants you to stop using the word."

"But that's absurd. We all know he's a ghost. Why shouldn't we call him one?"

"He wants you to call him an angel. He likes that word much better."

"I've had enough of this foolishness," Kent interrupted. "We came out here on the pretext of fishing, not to discuss the contents of my personal chest. Now, since your little game is obviously failing, I suggest we do something with this fish. We can't just leave him lying there on the bottom of the boat."

Arline opened the rented tackle box and removed the stringer. "Here," she said, handing it to Bruce. "Take the hook out of his mouth and put the fish on this stringer. By keeping him in he water, he'll stay fresh while you catch some more of his friends."

Bruce looked first at the stringer, then at the trout that was still very much alive and flopping. "Will he bite me?" Bruce asked. "If I try to pick him up, I mean."

Arline couldn't help it. She broke out laughing so hard she couldn't even answer at first. "No, he won't bite," she managed at last. "I'll string this one for you, to show you how it's done. But if you catch any more, you're on your own."

Both men watched as Arline removed the hook, then put the stringer through the fish's mouth and gill. After securing one end of the stringer to the boat, she tossed the fish back into the lake.

Bruce sat looking at her as she rinsed her hands in the water and wiped them dry on a towel that had been provided with the rest of the fishing gear. "You're quite a woman, Arline," he said. "I can see I have much to learn from you."

"Thank you, Bruce." she replied. "I'll take that as a compliment. And just in case you're interested, I'm enjoying putting a little fun in your life. I'm glad I agreed to help Jason out with his assignment."

"What is it with you two?" Kent asked. "Why won't you get off the subject of this ghost? I'm beginning to think you both believe he is real."

"That's what we've been trying to tell you, Father," Bruce said patiently. "Much as I hate to admit it, he's here trying to help me out with a problem. You see, Jenice has refused to marry me unless I show her I can change. Jason has been given the assignment to help me prove I can change, so Jenice will become my wife. It seems the whole idea of helping me was Samantha's. She apparently chose Jason over me, in spite of the fact he was a ghost. But she still cared enough to want to spare me from being hurt too badly." Bruce had explained himself very calmly and clearly, he believed, to his father, and now looked at him expectantly. "Wasn't that nice of Samantha?" he added, and then held his breath when Kent exploded.

"What?! Now you're telling me Samantha is a ghost, too? Now I know you've lost your senses, Bruce. I think it's time I come out of retirement and spend a little time with you."

"You want to spend time with me now?" Bruce looked at his father curiously. "Why didn't you do that twenty years ago, when I wanted you to?"

Kent was silent for a long time before he spoke. "Are you trying to say I was a bad father for not spending time with you when you were a boy?"

Bruce shook his head. "I'm not saying you were a bad father. I know you loved me and always took care of me. You did take the time to help me get established in my profession. But still . . ."

"But still what?" Kent probed. "We both know you were different from most boys, Bruce. You never had time to be a child. There were times I wished you had been more like a regular boy instead of being so mature."

"I don't know what you're talking about, Father. I would have given anything to have had you take me fishing like this when I was a boy. Why did you think I wouldn't?"

Kent seldom smiled, but now his face bore traces of a deeper frown than usual. "Perhaps it was my mistake. I was so busy providing for you and your mother that I seem to have missed something even more important."

Jason, who had returned in time to hear the last of the conversation between Bruce and Kent, spoke to Arline. "I think the problem between these two goes deeper than either of them realizes. I saw the contents of the chest."

"Hold it, you two," Arline said, holding out both hands for emphasis. "Jason just got back, and I think he has something important to say."

"Did he see inside the chest?" Bruce asked anxiously.

"He did. But I refuse to ask him what he found there until I have your word you'll call him an angel from now on."

"You have my word, Jason. If you can really tell me what's inside my father's chest, I'll never refer to you as a gho— , well you know what I mean. I'll call you an angel, okay?"

Jason looked at Arline. "I think Bruce is in for a shock, Arline. The chest is filled with memories of a little boy. On the top is a time-worn copy of Eugene Field's poem, 'Little Boy Blue.'"

"Are you kidding me?" Arline stared at Kent. "You have a copy of Eugene Field's 'Little Boy Blue' in your chest?"

Kent suddenly went pale. "How could you know that?" he stammered.

"Jason told me. He also said the chest is filled with memories of a little boy." Arline tried to speak gently.

Jason added, "Tell him there's a set of wooden bookends apparently made in grade school. They're inscribed with the words 'I love you, Daddy.'"

Arline felt a lump in her throat. "Jason tells me there is a set of wooden bookends with 'I love you, Daddy' inscribed on them," she said softly.

Bruce looked at his father in surprise. "Are those the bookends I made for you when I was in the sixth grade, Father?"

Kent looked stunned. "I don't understand. How did you manage to get into my trunk?"

"We didn't," Arline explained. "It was Jason."

"Then—there really is a . . . ?"

"Call him an *angel*, Father," Bruce said proudly. "So you saved those old bookends all these years. You didn't even like them when I gave them to you. I had hoped you would use them in your office, but they just disappeared."

"Where is the ghost now?" Kent demanded.

"He's sitting here right next to me," Arline laughed.

"I assure you, Father, he means you no harm," Bruce added. "Now tell me about the bookends. Why do you have them in the chest?"

"You're not lying to me? There really is a ghost named Jason here with us now?" Kent pressed.

"He's not only here with us, but he's turning out to be a better friend to me than I had ever supposed."

Kent sighed and rubbed his chin. "I never used your bookends, son" he explained, "because I didn't want them to get damaged. They were too important to me. Have either of you ever read Eugene Field's poem?" he asked. Bruce shook his head no.

"I read it in high school," Arline said.

"I can quote it to you now, if you like," Kent volunteered.

"You've memorized the whole poem?" she asked.

Kent drew in a deep breath. "I've dropped off to sleep so many times quoting it to myself, I've long since lost count." He looked directly at Bruce as he began the poem:

> The little toy dog is covered with dust, but sturdy and staunch he stands;
> And the little toy soldier is red with rust, and his musket molds in his hands.
> Time was when the little toy dog was new, and the soldier was passing fair,
> And that was the time when our Little Boy Blue kissed them and put them there.
> "Now don't you go till I come," he said, "and don't you make any noise!"
> So toddling off to his trundle-bed, he dreamed of the pretty toys.
> And as he was dreaming, an angel song awakened our Little Boy Blue—
> Oh, the years are many, the years are long, but the little toy friends are true.
> Ay, faithful to Little Boy Blue they stand, each in the same old place,
> Awaiting the touch of a little hand, the smile of a little face.
> And they wonder, as waiting these long years through, in the dust of that little chair,
> What has become of our Little Boy Blue since he kissed them and put them there.

Tears ran freely from Kent's eyes as he concluded the words of the poem. "I know our little boy blue wasn't called home by angels. But he was taken from us, nevertheless. I always assumed I had tomorrow to spend some time with you, Bruce. But tomorrow came more quickly than I realized, and before I knew it—it was too late. I've always wondered if you held it against me for not doing things with you that most boys like. But until now, I never knew for sure. You never let on like you wanted my attention, so I used that as an excuse. I concluded that you were more mature than most boys and understood why I had to spend my time working. I even eased my conscience by sending you to college to get the same training I had."

When Arline looked back to Bruce, he was crying, too. "We're a couple of fools, father," he said. "I always thought you wanted me to be different from the other boys, so I did my best to oblige you."

"Do you think it's too late for us to give it a try?" Kent asked hopefully.

"I suppose it's never too late, Father. What do you have in mind?"

"I was just thinking," Kent said, glancing back to Arline. "Since Bruce is trying to make some changes in his life, maybe I could join in, too. Do you suppose your angel friend could help me catch a fish of my own? I mean, while I'm explaining the rest of the things I've kept in my chest, that is."

"I can't believe this," Jason said to a smiling Arline. "You're making some good progress here. There may be hope for this wim— uh, I mean, guy yet. I'll be glad to help them with their father-and-son fishing trip."

Both men caught their limit that day, but none of the other fish was quite as large as the first one. That night, for the evening meal, Arline prepared the best trout any of them had ever tasted. Jason showed her how, of course.

CHAPTER ELEVEN

A quick glance at his watch told Fred it was twenty minutes past midnight. By this time the office complex would be empty. Fortune was on Fred's side in that no one had thought of calling in his keys when he was fired. It was the realization that he still had the keys that first gave Fred the idea for his plan. If everything went as it should, Fred figured he still had a good shot at the talk show that Arline had cheated him out of.

Moving to the double glass entrance doors, Fred stared inside at the security station. Sure enough, old Frank was asleep. Everyone knew Frank spent most of his shift asleep, but Stewart didn't have the heart to dismiss the man. He had been a fixture in the organization for more than twenty years and had been a close friend of Stewart's father.

Fred slid his key into the lock and turned it ever so quietly. Once the door was open, he slinked past the security station and around the corner to the back stairway. It was even easier than he had hoped. Quickly making his way to the third floor, he stopped at the door marked "Stewart Carson." Just as he had expected, he found Stewart's door unlocked. Stewart Carson was a man of habit, one of which was never locking doors. Fred switched on the light and glanced at the bookcase on the back wall. There he spotted what he was looking for. It was the coveted "Golfer of the Year" award, presented to Stewart last May when he won his fifth straight Broadcaster Executives tournament. The two-foot-high trophy, which depicted a golfer with readied club, was one of Stewart's most treasured possessions. Given the choice between playing golf or winning the state lottery, Stewart would pick golf every time.

Cramming the award into a canvas bag he had brought along,

Fred made his way quickly to the door. He paused and looked back over the office. Then, just for good measure, he set the canvas bag next to the door and ransacked everything in sight. When he was finished, Stewart's office looked as if a cyclone had passed through it.

Getting out of the building was even easier than getting in. Once back in his truck, Fred found his cousin Andrew waiting nervously inside.

Fred smiled. "Take it easy, Andy," he said. "Everything went fine, just like I said it would. You have absolutely nothing to worry about. And when this is over, I give you my word, I'll call our debt even. Help me out with this one, and you'll be free of me forever. Let me down, and you can guess what will happen, can't you?"

Andrew didn't look happy. "Why does all this sound so familiar? Let me guess. It's because you told me the exact same thing when I agreed to help you rig the contest with Arline Wilson. You said nothing could go wrong that time, too. Not to mention your promise to leave me alone after helping you with that one."

"All right, Andy, I made a mistake. Something went wrong, okay? I still can't figure out what happened. But that job is rightfully mine, and I intend to have it. This time will be different. I've planned out every little detail. I'm absolutely certain there's no room left for error with this one."

"This is kidnapping, Fred. Do you know what they do to kidnappers?"

"Don't think of it as kidnapping, Cousin Andy. What we're really doing is apprehending a criminal. When this is over, we'll be heros—not kidnappers. But so help me, Andy, if you do anything to foul up this deal—anything at all—I'll see to it that picture gets into the right hands—"

Andrew interrupted him. "What you're doing to me is wrong, Fred, and you know it. I had no idea what those guys were up to that night. I thought they just liked my car and wanted to go for a spin."

"You and I know that, Andy. But the police won't know it. If they see the picture of that gang sitting in front of the bank they robbed, with Andy Whitlock at the wheel, what conclusion do you think they'll draw?"

"You never have told me how you happened to get that cursed

picture in the first place. As long as you plan on blackmailing me with it the rest of my life, don't you think it would be fair to tell me how you came by it?"

Fred shrugged. "You know me, Andy. I'm the luckiest man in the county. Always have been and always will be. When a fellow's born with the gift of luck, he never loses it. I'd just bought the camera at Johnson's Photo Shop, right across the street from the bank. I no more than stepped out the front door of the shop when who do I see in his shiny new Ford Escort but good old Cousin Andy. How was I to know I was photographing the getaway car for a bank holdup? Since they later caught the real gang, I never saw any need to show the picture to anyone. Especially since I knew you were innocent, cousin."

"You didn't show it to the authorities because you knew you could use it to blackmail me into doing whatever you might want," Andrew grumbled.

"Well, that might have been part of my motive," Fred admitted genially. "I have to admit, it has come in handy several times."

"And of course this will be the last time you ever use it, right?"

"You have my absolute word of honor on that, Andy. If I'm not telling the truth, may I take the blame for driving the gang at that holdup myself."

"Fat chance of that ever happening," Andrew snorted. "So what does your new foolproof plan call for us to do next?"

Fred started his truck, backed it out of the parking space, and headed for the parking lot exit. "We wait for just the right moment," he said. "When that moment comes, we tamper with destiny, cousin. Once we get destiny reshaped to the way it ought to be, I'll be signing autographs for little old ladies, Andy. Lots of little old ladies."

CHAPTER TWELVE

Arline held her breath and wondered in her heart if Bruce could gather the courage to leave the security of the plane and leap into the emptiness of the early morning sky. It had taken a great deal of effort and self-discipline on his part to get him to the point of crouching in the open doorway of the Cessna, some 3,000 feet above the brightly painted target of Rudolph Pepperdine's Skydiving school.

"You can do it!" Arline yelled, her voice barely audible above the roar of passing wind and engine noise. "You have to do it! There are only two days left until you do it for real, over Howard Placard's private beach."

"He'll never do it," Jason chuckled. "I have to admit he's come a lot further than I ever thought he could in the time you've been working with him, but he'll never jump out of this airplane. Look at his knuckles, Arline. They're turning white from gripping the safety rail so hard."

Arline knew Jason was right. Bruce had come a long way in the past few weeks, but jumping from a plane was a huge step beyond anything he had accomplished so far. With mounting tension, Arline waited on Bruce's decision and let thoughts of the last three weeks drift through her mind. The fishing trip with his father had been a major turning point for Bruce. From that point on, his determination had shot skyward. It was as though he found himself that day in the rowboat and for the first time in his life knew exactly who he was. Convincing Bruce to take a full leave of absence from his practice had been much easier than Arline had thought it would be, and it had opened the door for one new experience after another.

The look on Ted Freeman's face when Bruce and Arline had actually showed up at his house to take him up on the offer of borrowing two motorcycles was one Arline would never forget. "This is mind-crushing astonishment!" he exclaimed. "I never thought I'd see the day when Bruce would ride anything wilder than a chair at the Hunter's Cottage dining room. I've missed hearing you on the radio, Arline. But I have to say if spending your vacation time with Bruce has brought him to this, maybe you should take another month or two. I think there's hope for this guy yet."

True, the Honda 90 Bruce rode for the day was a far cry from Ted's Kawasaki, but there was no denying that a new Bruce emerged from the adventure. After mustering the courage to climb his first hill, Arline wondered if she had created a monster. Even after falling off the bike time and time again, Bruce had to be forced to give it up as the sun lowered into the late afternoon sky.

If Ted could have seen Bruce the following day, he would have been stunned for sure. Despite every muscle in his body aching from the motorcycle venture, he had agreed to Arline's suggestion they rent a boat and try his hand at waterskiing. Arline was beginning to question her wisdom in suggesting this adventure when after more than fifteen attempts Bruce still had not managed to come up on the skis. She even wondered if his technique of skiing on his face could be patented. On the next try, however, he made it. Never could she remember feeling so proud as she did watching him skip along over the ripples with that look of complete triumph on his face.

Arline especially enjoyed the hike to the top of Red Rock Peak, where they spent the evening overlooking the panoramic view of the city at night. The afternoon at the zoo was nice, too. Bruce had shocked her by admitting it was his first time ever to see a zoo. Then there was the evening they rented a canoe and had a moonlight picnic on Dove Park Island. But the greatest surprise of all came when Bruce actually rode the dreaded roller-coaster. Of course, he went home sick that night, but he rode the thing nevertheless.

Arline couldn't help but be amazed at the progress Bruce had made. Like a feather on the wind, he flowed from one new experience to another. And much to her delight, he kept his word about not referring to Jason as a ghost. Jason, on the other hand, slipped a time or two on his end of the bargain. But for the most part, he did okay.

"Take it easy, mac," Rudolph Pepperdine yelled to Bruce. "Your parachute will be activated automatically. That's what this static line attached to the plane is for. All you have to do is close your eyes and think of yourself as stepping off the edge of your bed."

"Stepping off the edge of my bed?" Bruce echoed with a voice like jello. "Why would I ever want to step off the edge of my bed?"

"It doesn't matter that you'd never actually step off the edge of your bed, mac. Thinking of your first jump that way just makes it a little easier is all. It takes your mind off what you're really doing."

"This is crazy. Why did I have to fall in love with a woman like Jenice in the first place? Why couldn't I have fallen in love with a woman who gets her thrills from knitting socks or painting pictures of evening sunsets?"

"That's easy to understand," Jason laughed. "Any woman who likes to knit, or paint for that matter, would have to have good eyes. Why would a woman with good eyes ever take a second look at you, Bruce?"

"Listen, mac," Rudolph went on to say, "the parachute you're wearing is state-of-the-art. I've given you plenty of instructions on how to maneuver it during your descent. I'll be talking to you the whole time over the two-way radio. In three to five minutes it'll be all over, and you'll be safe on the ground. There's absolutely nothing to worry about."

"He's right, Bruce," Jason agreed. "There is nothing to worry about. Being dead is a real kick. I wouldn't have it any other way now that I've gotten used to it. Why not give the old boy a push, Arline? No, come to think of it, that wouldn't work, either. Knowing Bruce, he'd be so scared he'd take half the side of the plane with him."

"Will you shut up!" Arline scolded. "This is tough enough without your interference."

Rudolph moved into the opening next to Bruce. "Okay, mac," he said. "This is it. I'll be right beside you all the way. Now I'm going to count to three, and we jump. Ready? One, two . . ."

* * *

"What do you suppose they're doing up there, Fred?" Andrew

asked as the two of them stood outside the white pickup truck, straining to see the plane overhead.

"Believe me, Andy, I have no idea. This new boyfriend of Arline's is a real fruitcake. I've done some checking on him, and he's a wealthy psychologist. Maybe he just wants to take up skydiving. Who knows?"

"Well whatever it is they're doing, it's obvious we can't get to Arline as long as she's flying around like a bird in the sky. I vote we give up on this outlandish idea of yours, Fred. Let's go home and forget the whole thing while there's still time."

"How many times do I have to tell you, knothead, we're not giving up on this? It's imperative I keep Arline from meeting with Stewart Carson tomorrow afternoon. When she fails to show up for the appointment, it won't take long for Stewart to start looking for someone else to fill that television slot—especially when we put part two of my plan in place. And when he starts looking for her replacement, I'll be the natural one for him to turn to. They can't stay up there in that airplane all day, and when they come down, we'll just have to find a way of getting Arline's boyfriend out of the picture long enough to grab her."

"I'd like to know how you expect to get the boyfriend out of the picture," Andrew argued. "Those two have been staying closer than syrup on a Belgium waffle the last few weeks. It's going to take a major event to get them apart."

Fred's eyes suddenly lit up as his lips curled into a crafty grin. "You're right, Andy," he said. "And we're the ones who can make that major event come about. Come on, we've got work to do."

* * *

"It's no use," Bruce moaned, as he pulled off his parachute and fell backward into his seat. "I just can't do it. I don't know what I'm going to do if I lose Jenice, but I just can't bring myself to step out of the plane."

Arline slid to the seat next to Bruce and took hold of his hand. "We still have two days," she comforted. "We can try again tomorrow. We'll do it right after my interview with Stewart Carson."

"I'm sorry, mac," Rudolph said, removing his own chute. "I can teach you the ropes, but I can't give you the fortitude to use what you know. It's up to you to make the jump. Right now, we've got to get this plane on the ground. I have another paying customer scheduled to make a jump in less than twenty minutes. If you want to try again tomorrow, I'll work you in."

"Yes, of course," Bruce acknowledged. "We'll try again tomorrow."

The screeching sound of rubber against the concrete runway told Arline the plane had touched down. As the craft slowed in speed and turned toward the hanger next to Rudolph's office, something caught her attention.

"Look, Bruce," she exclaimed. "Isn't that Ted Freeman riding up on his red Kawasaki?"

"Yes, Bruce replied. "It is Ted. I wonder what he's doing here."

"You know Ted Freeman?" Rudolph asked. "Ted's one of my regulars. He's an advanced student of mine. Ted jumps three to four times every week. If he's a friend of yours, maybe you can get him to help you pull up enough gumption to make that first jump."

"I could give him enough gumption to make the first jump," Jason snickered. "If I only had hands to push him out the door."

The engines ground to a standstill, and everyone except the pilot climbed out of the plane. By this time Ted had parked his motorcycle next to Rudolph's office and was walking in their direction.

"If it ain't Bruce Vincent," he called as he spotted Bruce with his unused parachute. "When did you take up the sport?"

Bruce let out a slow lingering sigh. "I'm afraid I haven't exactly taken up the sport yet, Ted. I made it as far as looking out the open door of the plane, but that first step has eluded me, I fear. Perhaps you can give me some pointers that will help me go through with it next time."

Ted laughed. "Hey man, you just do it. That's the secret to everything in this life. Never show fear, and just do it. It works every time."

"I'll try to remember that next time," Bruce replied with a forced smile. "Would you like to use this parachute?" he asked, extending the chute toward Ted. "I assure you, it's none the worse for wear for my having taken it on a plane ride."

"Thanks, Bruce, but I have my own chute inside in a locker. That's another secret of life—always use the best equipment, and always fold your own parachute. That way I have a better chance of living to jump again next time." Then, turning to Rudolph, Ted asked, "Who belongs to the great-looking red convertible over there, man?"

"That," Arline answered before Rudolph could respond, "is Bruce's new transportation. I picked it out for him. Do you like it?"

"That's your car, Bruce? I'm impressed. But I think you should know, when I was riding up just now I saw those two guys in that white pickup over there messing around the car. You'd better check it out good before you leave. My guess is they were looking to take it on a trip to the market—in Old Mexico."

"You mean you think they were trying to steal my car?"

"Yeah, I think so. I'm not sure how far they would have gotten if I hadn't interrupted them, but you may find it's been broken into."

"Thanks, Ted," Bruce said, as he and Arline started off in the direction of his car. "I will check it out. And I hope you have more fun skydiving than I did."

"No sweat, man," Ted called back as he and Rudolph headed for the building. "That's another of life's secrets. No matter what else, always have fun."

"I'm glad that young fellow's not a few years older," Jason observed. "If he was, and if Jenice ever met up with him, Bruce would be left holding an unused ring at the altar for sure. The word 'wimp' just doesn't seem to come to mind around that guy."

At first glance everything seemed in order when they reached the car, but as Bruce rounded to the far side, he was surprised to find two tires had been flattened.

"Would you look at this?" he exclaimed. "If they wanted to steal the car, why would they flatten the tires? They must be a couple of young pranksters or something."

"I'm not sure about that, Bruce," Arline responded as she got a closer look at the white pickup. "That looks a lot like Fred Goodson's truck. Fred's the one I told you about. He was fired when he tried to rig the contest Stewart Carson had set up between us. Why don't you go inside and call the police while I stay here with your car?"

"That might not be a bad idea," Bruce agreed. "I'll need to call the auto club, too, to get these tires repaired. But don't you think it would be better if you come inside with me, just to be on the safe side?"

"No way, Bruce. If that is Fred over there, I want to know what he's up to. You go make the calls. I'll wait here and keep an eye on him."

Bruce glanced again toward the two men sitting in the white pickup. "I don't know," he said uneasily. "I'd just feel better if you come along with me. I really don't like the looks of those two."

Arline put her hands on her hips. "Bruce Vincent, you're not my mother. I remember Sam telling me how you always treated her like a child. I can tell you right now, that kind of attitude will get you nowhere but in deep trouble with a woman like Jenice. Now go make your phone calls. I'll be fine."

"Very well, Arline," Bruce relented, as he started back toward the building. "But I don't like it."

As Bruce stepped inside the office he found Rudolph at his desk filling out a flight log. Ted was in the back of the room, removing some paraphernalia from a locker. Both men immediately looked up as Bruce entered the room.

"I think you were right about those men," Bruce said. "I found two of my tires flattened. May I use your phone, Rudolph?"

Even before the jump instructor could reply, all three men were startled by Arline's scream. Bruce was first out the door, with the other two right behind. They were just in time to see Arline pushed into the pickup truck and squeezed between the two men. Bruce watched helplessly as the truck shot into motion, the gravel from the unpaved parking area flying wildly rearward in a cloud of dust. Glancing first at his disabled car, then at the rapidly vanishing truck, Bruce turned and slammed a fist into the side of the building.

"Why didn't I force her to come inside with me?" he exclaimed. Just at that moment, the bright red Kawasaki parked only a few feet away caught his eye. Frozen in a mixture of urgent distress and cold terror, Bruce stared at the machine. Riding a Honda 90 was one thing, but thoughts of mounting a bike the size of this one left him in a cold sweat. Then, forcing out some of the hardest words of his life, he shouted, "The keys, Ted! Give me the keys to your motor-cycle!"

"My motorcycle? Now, wait a minute, Bruce!"

"I'll buy the thing from you for twice what it's worth! Just give me those keys NOW!"

Digging deep in his pocket, Ted retrieved the keys and placed them in Bruce's shaking hand. "You don't have to buy it," he stammered. "Just don't let those guys get away."

The engine on the big bike roared into life. An unbelievably pale Bruce forced his foot hard against the shift lever, released the clutch, and let out a panicked cry that could be heard several decibels above the sound of the screaming exhaust. Fishtailing wildly onto the pavement, Bruce fought to bring the machine under control. Then, in an instant, he was speeding toward the road ahead, in hot pursuit of the now distant white pickup truck. His only hope, since the truck was no longer in sight, was that they stayed on the main road until he could catch up with them.

* * *

"What do you think you're doing, Fred Goodson?" Arline shrieked. "This is kidnapping! You can't get away with this!"

"That's what you think, lady," Fred retorted sharply. "By the time I'm finished, you'll be the one the authorities will be looking for. And you can kiss that television talk show goodbye in the bargain. If it hadn't been for your interference, the job would have been mine in the first place. All I'm doing is putting things straight again."

Arline struggled to free her hands, which had been tied behind her back. "Is that what this is all about?" she cried out in disgust. "If you'll remember, Fred, it was you who made every effort to get the job by deception. I won it fairly because I was the most qualified."

"Most qualified? Ha! The only way you could have beaten me out of that job was by using your feminine charms to sway Carson's mind to your side."

"My feminine charms?" Arline twisted to glare at Fred. "What exactly are you accusing me of, Fred Goodson?"

"You know perfectly well what I'm accusing you of. And we both know it's true. Otherwise, Carson would never have taken a second look at the likes of you."

"You'll pay for this, Fred!" Arline fumed. "I can promise you that much. I'll see to it you rue the day you ever dreamed up a rotten scheme like this one."

Fred chuckled. "You'll make me pay? I think not. By the time this is over, you'll be in no position to make anyone pay."

"Hang in there, Arline," Jason consoled. "This guy likes to break all the rules, but he has no idea what he's up against this time. I may not be able to punch him out, but I'm not exactly helpless, either. We'll get you out of this in one piece, I give you my word. And if it's any comfort, Bruce is right behind you on Ted's Kawasaki."

"He's what?" Arline shouted. "Good grief—he'll be killed!"

"Who'll be killed?" A confused scowl replaced Fred's confident smile. "What are you talking about? Oh, don't tell me," he said as he grinned. "You're talking to your imaginary ghost, right? I'm beginning to think you actually believe the guy's here. I'm doing the people of this town a bigger service than I supposed. At least now they'll be spared a talk show hostess who talks to Casper's big brother."

"Believe it or not," Jason went on to say, "Bruce is doing a pretty good job keeping the big bike on the road. I've never seen him more terrified, but at least he hasn't fallen off yet. See if you can learn where these guys are taking you. It'll give me something to work with until I can come up with a way to get you free from them."

"I assume you know where you're taking me, Fred," Arline asked, following Jason's suggestion. "Would it be putting you out too much to let me in on the secret?"

"You're going on a train ride. That's all you need to know right now."

"A train ride?" Jason pondered aloud. "I spent twenty years of my life—so to speak—in this vicinity, and I can't think of any railroads around here. See if you can get any more than that out of him."

"What kind of train ride?" Arline pressed. "There aren't any railroads around these parts."

"I told you all I'm going to for now! Just shut up and behave yourself like a good little girl, or I'll really make things rough on you."

"You're just trying to make me miss my appointment with Stewart Carson tomorrow afternoon, aren't you?" Arline accused him.

"Well, would you get a load of this?" Fred sneered. "We have a real lady Einstein in our midst. I'm amazed. I had no idea she was that intelligent."

At that moment, Arline managed to get her hands free from the knotted handkerchief Fred and Andrew had used to tie her. In one quick motion, she crammed her foot against the brake pedal and switched off the ignition. Before Andrew could recover, she reached across and unlatched the door on his side. Using all her weight, she shoved him out the door. Then, leaping from the truck, Arline ran from the scene as fast as her legs would carry her. She might have gotten away with it if it hadn't been for her shoes. Of all the stupid things to wear for an airplane ride. Why hadn't she gone with the casual pants outfit and flats she had almost worn that morning, instead of the red dress and high heels? She berated herself as Fred and Andrew dragged her back to the truck.

At least her effort accomplished one thing. By the time the two men had her back in the truck and they were again under way, Bruce had managed to pull within sight. Fortunately, he was able to see them turn onto the dirt road, heading north toward the mountains.

* * *

Choking on the heavy cloud of dust raised by the fast-moving truck was no fun, but Bruce refused to give up the chase.

It was a toss-up which had the most to do with his missing the turn—the dust or his inexperience on the bike. He missed it, nevertheless, and soon found himself flying headlong over the handlebars onto a ledge of soft sand in the center of Henderson Creek. The motorcycle came to a stop a few feet away in the shallow water at the edge of the creek. It took only a moment's evaluation to realize the predicament he was in. The hill back to the road was much too sandy and steep for him to push the heavy bike up. On the other hand, he had little confidence of being able to ride it up the hill.

"Bruce, you idiot," he scolded himself. "You've really done it this time. If you don't find a way to get that motorcycle back on the road,

Arline will be at the mercy of those scoundrels." Pulling the bike back onto its wheels, he put every ounce of strength in his body into an attempt to push it back up the hill.

* * *

Arline knew they must be getting close to some kind of civilization when she heard the deep barking of a dog. Sure enough, as they rounded one last curve, there he was. He appeared to be an older bloodhound, and from all appearances seemed friendly enough. Next, she caught sight of a small, well-kept house trailer situated under the shade of two huge cottonwood trees.

As Fred brought the truck to a stop, a short pudgy man dressed in overalls stepped out of the trailer and made his way toward them. His smile seemed out of place for the occasion, Arline thought. It was almost as if he were expecting guests for dinner rather than assisting in a kidnapping. Arline wondered if Fred had somehow tricked the man into thinking nothing was amiss in them bringing her here. She understood Fred well enough to know that was a definite possibility.

"Afternoon, Fred," the man said as he drew near. "I see you brought Andrew along. Is this here the lady you was telling me about?"

"This is her, Uncle Elmo," Fred answered as he opened the door and stepped down from the truck.

In the meantime, Andrew opened his door and stepped out also, dragging Arline out behind him. "Hi ya, Uncle Elmo," he said. "It's been a while, hasn't it?"

"Yes, son, it has been a while at that. I'm a little surprised to see you hanging around Fred here. I thought the two of you parted company long ago."

"It's not like I haven't tried to stay clear of him, Uncle. He just sort of has this magnetic hold on me and won't let go." Andrew threw a glance toward Fred, who only scowled at him.

"Is the old engine fired up and ready to go, Uncle?" Fred asked.

"Well, now, young man, she's not fired up just yet. But I can have her under way in less time than it takes you to say your prayers at night. And in your case, Fred, that's pretty darn fast. You said there would be another fellow along, you know, to do the . . ." Elmo moved a hand to hide his lips from Arline as he mouthed the word *"proposing."*

"Oh, yeah, well, he'll be along later. Right now, we have to get the woman up the mountain, so why don't you go get that engine fired up and ready to go?"

"This answers the question of the railroad," Jason said, after looking the place over good. "There's a train parked in a big red barn out back of the old man's trailer."

"What about—you know . . . ?" Arline asked, trying not to reveal the fact they were being followed.

"Bruce is having a bit of a transportation problem at the moment. I'll keep you posted when there's a change."

"Transportation problem?" Arline asked anxiously. "He's not hurt, is he?"

"Only his pride, Arline."

Elmo pulled off his engineer's cap and scratched the back of his head. "Who's she talking to?" he asked.

"Don't pay any attention to her, Uncle Elmo," Fred responded. "She's a little touched in the head. Thinks she's being haunted by some ghost named Jason."

"Is that right, missy? You talk to one of them ghosts, do you?" Arline glared at the man but didn't answer. "No need to be unfriendly," Elmo said when he saw her intention. "I didn't mean to imply I disbelieved you or nothing. In fact, I've see a couple of ghosts myself up at the old lodge. Never talked to one, though."

"Listen, Elmo—that is your name I assume," Arline said forcefully. "I don't know what Fred has told you, but I assure you I'm here against my will. So unless you want to be part of a kidnapping, I suggest you help me get away from these two bozos."

"Oh, yes, ma'am," Elmo replied with a wink at Fred. "I know all about your being kidnapped. Sure is a terrible thing, isn't it?"

"Bring the woman and come on," Fred called back to the others as he started off in the direction of the building where the train was kept. "We've talked enough. I've got a lot of ground to cover yet today."

Tightening his grip on Arline's arm, Andrew forced her to follow after Fred. Suddenly Jason, who had disappeared moments earlier, was alongside her again.

"I've checked things out," he explained. "There's a set of tracks leading up the mountain to a big empty lodge. That must be where they're taking you. There's two things I need you to do. First, I want you to drop something from your purse that the bloodhound can get your scent from. And next, I need you to find out the dog's name. I'm sure he knows I'm here, and I might be able to use him to get a message across to Bruce, if he ever catches up."

"Ow!" Arline cried out as she fell to the ground, faking a twisted ankle. "You're forcing me to walk too fast in these heels."

Fred quickly moved in to help Andrew get Arline back to her feet. "Cut the theatrics," he barked. "You're nowhere near ready for the Academy Awards with an act like that." As they moved on, her lipstick tube lay unnoticed on the spot where she had fallen.

It took nearly ten minutes for Elmo to get Engine 707 up to steam. Fred gave him a hand while Andrew held tight to Arline.

"Are you in on this because you want to be, Andrew?" Arline asked as they waited. "Or has old Fred found a way to trick you into helping him out? He is your cousin, I presume. I heard you call him 'cousin.'"

Andrew grimaced. "Fred's my cousin, all right. And no, I don't want to be a party to this, but he can ruin me for life if I don't go along with his plan."

"He's going to prison for this, you know. And unless you convince me not to press charges against you, guess who his cellmate will be for the next twenty years?"

"No! He's promised that won't happen. I'm sorry for whatever happens to you, Arline, but I can't cross Fred. He has me in a corner."

"The dog's name," Jason interrupted. "Get him to tell you the dog's name. I'll need to know it if I'm going to make my plan work."

"That dog over there, Andrew. Does he belong to your Uncle Elmo?"

"Old Rastus? Yeah, he's my uncle's dog. Why?"

"I happen to like dogs," Arline said casually. "When the three of you are taken into custody, someone will have to look out for him. If it's me, I need to know his name."

"Stop saying things like that. Fred will keep anything from happening to me. He's given me his word."

"I'd sure hate to have my future depending on the word of a man like Fred. Help me out here, Andrew, and I give you my word not to press charges against you."

"You don't understand, Arline. I can't do that. Now stop pressuring me."

"All right, Andy," Fred called out as he approached the two of them again. "You can ride with her in the coach. I'm going to stay with Uncle Elmo so I can brush up on how to run this rig. He doesn't know it yet, but I intend to bring it down the mountain without him."

The quiet of the peaceful mountain day was broken by the shrill whistle of the old steamer. At first the iron engine wheels slipped noisily against the rails, but they quickly took hold, bringing the little train into motion for the trip up the hill. With steam bellowing out from both sides, the powerful engine soon had them up to thirty miles an hour as they disappeared around the first bend.

* * *

Bruce soon realized it was useless trying to push the motorcycle up the hill. And so, gathering all the courage he could, he started the engine. Slipping the bike into first gear, he said a quick prayer and let out the clutch. The bike shot forward in a burst of power that pulled the front wheel clear of the ground. With the rear wheel spinning madly while throwing gravel a hundred feet behind, the whole scene seemed to shift into slow motion. Inch by terrifying inch, the bike moved upward, until a thousand heartbeats later, it suddenly caught hold and burst over the top, completely airborne. Too frightened to let up on the throttle, man and machine hit the ground running. In his wildest nightmares Bruce had never found himself in such a perilous situation. Still, he clung on with all his might and guided the large motorcycle down the dirt road at a speed that he hoped would make up for lost time.

The first thing coming into view as he rounded the curve was the white pickup truck. Bruce quickly brought the big bike to a standstill and took stock of the situation. Seeing that the truck was empty, Bruce parked the motorcycle and rushed to the house trailer, only to find it deserted as well.

"Where are they?" he cried frantically. "How could they have disappeared so completely?" Then, he caught a glimpse of the old bloodhound out behind the trailer. The dog was acting very unusual.

"Here, boy," Jason called out, trying to get the dog's attention. "Come on, Rastus, let's have a big jump. And make some noise while you're at it."

"Ruff," the dog growled while looking at Jason, who was holding his hand up in an attempt to get the animal to stand on his rear legs.

"Come on, boy, you can do it," Jason continued to encourage, moving his hand in a circular motion. In spite of his advanced age, old Rastus couldn't resist a good game when offered. With one quick lunge, he was up barking at Jason's moving hand.

It took Bruce only a few seconds to figure out what was happening.

"Jason, it's you, isn't it? You're using the dog to get my attention. Get him to turn around in a circle, and I'll know for sure it's you."

"Way to go, Bruce," Jason shouted. "You figured out my plan perfectly. Come on, Rastus, let's do a few spins."

As Bruce watched in amazement, Rastus did several full spins. "I knew it! It is you! Can you figure a way to show me where they've taken Arline?"

In an instant, the dog was off on a dead run in the direction of the red building where the train had been. Bruce was quick to follow.

"Here, Rastus," Jason said, pointing to Arline's lipstick, which lay where she had dropped it. Rastus came to a stop and put his nose to the object, which Bruce picked up as soon as he reached it.

"It's Arline's," Bruce exclaimed. "I've seen her use it. Here, boy, get a good whiff of her scent," he said holding the tube out toward the bloodhound. "Now," Bruce said, after he was sure the dog had the scent, "go find her, boy."

With one deep rolling bark, Rastus was off toward the iron railroad tracks leading up the mountain. Once he reached the tracks, the dog followed them for several feet, then stopped and barked loudly toward Bruce.

"They're on a train?" Bruce asked aloud. Then, looking more closely at the tracks, he could see signs of water droplets from the condensing steam, clinging to the rocks and bushes on the ground.

"Jason," he cried out. "If Arline's on a train headed up these tracks, get the dog to show me somehow."

Getting Rastus to chase him up the tracks was an easy matter for Jason, and it was all the sign Bruce needed. Two minutes later he was maneuvering the Kawasaki up the mountain, staying in the middle of the tracks. It was a bumpy ride to say the least, but this didn't distract him one bit.

"I can't believe this," Jason said in amazement. "Who is this guy? And what has he done with the real Bruce Vincent?"

CHAPTER THIRTEEN

Under different circumstances, the train ride up the mountain could have been a pleasant experience. The constant sound of the wheels clicking over the iron rails, along with an occasional blast from the steam whistle, lulled Arline's mind into a time long gone by—a time when the pace of life was slower and filled with rich opportunity to enjoy the simple things man and nature combined to offer. Mountain scenery in unimaginable splendor passed majestically by her window mile after fascinating mile. Unfortunately, the grandeur of it all remained hidden behind the grim reality of the reason she was here.

Turning her attention to Andrew, who was seated in the chair next to hers, Arline couldn't help but notice his nervous tension. She was sure both Andrew and the one they called Uncle Elmo were in on this kidnapping for reasons other than Fred Goodson's. Somehow, Fred had entrapped them into their parts in the scheme. If she played her hand just right, she reasoned there was a good chance of winning the help of one, or perhaps both of these men. Suddenly, she was pulled from her state of deep thought by the sound of Jason's voice.

"It worked, Arline. I was able to use old Rastus to get my message across to Bruce. I wish you could see the old boy right now. You'd never believe it. He's not more than ten miles behind the train, having the ride of his life on the Kawasaki. I still can't believe the change in that guy. A month ago I'd have given you odds the moon would fall from the sky before Bruce would do something like this."

"I only hope he comes through for me," Arline answered. "If I don't show up for that interview with Stewart Carson tomorrow . . ."

"You'll make the interview, I promise. If Bruce fails to come through, I'll think of something. I sure do wish Gus were here, though. Being an angel in this world is like being an eagle without wings. Gus always took the place of those wings when I was here before. This time I'm on my own, and it's a little frightening."

"Are you talking to that ghost again?" Andrew asked anxiously.

"He's not a ghost. He's an angel. And he's in the process of contacting some more of his friends to help me out here. If you don't see to it I get to my appointment on time tomorrow, you're going to find yourself the target of a whole army of angels. And some of them are pretty mean and ugly, too."

Great beads of sweat popped out on Andrew's forehead as he slithered a little deeper into his seat. "Angels aren't real. You're only putting me on."

"Oh, Jason is real all right. I'll prove it to you, Andrew. Tell me the address of where you live, and I'll have him describe the place for you."

"How do I know you haven't seen my house before?"

"Okay then, think of something you have sitting in plain sight inside your house. You know for sure I've never been inside."

"I don't like this game. I wish you'd cut it out."

"You don't like the game, Andrew, because you're afraid you'll find out my angel is real. Wouldn't it better for you to find out how real he is right now, than later, when he comes back with an army?"

"I—I live at 9273 West Grant. I've been reading a book. I left it lying on the nightstand next to my bed this morning."

"You want to check out the name of that book, Jason?" Arline asked.

"I already have."

"You what? Just how fast can you travel, anyway?"

"Pretty fast, Arline. The name of the book is *How to Outsmart a Blackmailer.*"

"Blackmail? That's how Fred's forcing you to do his dirty work, isn't it? He's blackmailing you?"

"How do you know that?" Andrew screeched. "You're playing some kind of trick on me, I know."

"The only trick involved is my angel's ability to move about so quickly. He saw the book on your nightstand and told me it's about blackmail. What else did you see while you were there, Jason?"

"There's a silk robe lying on the foot of his bed. It has pink hearts all over it."

"You wear a silk robe with pink hearts on it, Andrew? I'd hate to think what your slippers must look like."

"The angel is real!" Andrew gulped. "You're not going to let him hurt me, are you?"

"That all depends on you," Arline answered. "Now tell me, what is it Fred is blackmailing you with?"

Andrew looked around nervously. "Where is the angel right now?" he asked.

Arline smiled. "He's sitting on your lap. Now answer my question about the blackmail."

"Sitting on his lap? Give me a break, Arline," Jason pleaded. "I mean, this guy wears a pink robe and you tell him I'm sitting on his lap?"

Andrew gulped and began talking rapidly. "I was tricked into being the getaway driver in a holdup a couple of years ago. I had no idea what those guys were doing in the bank, I swear. I thought I was just taking them for a joy ride in my new car. Of all things, Fred happened by and took a picture of me waiting in front of the bank with the robbers in the background. He's threatened to give the picture to the authorities if I don't help him keep you away from your interview tomorrow. And please, let me explain about the pink robe. My ten-year-old daughter gave it to me for my birthday. I hate the blasted thing, but I can't let her know that. So I wear it. What else can I do?"

Arline felt almost sorry for the man. "You may have been innocent of the bank robbery, Andrew, but you're stone guilty of kidnapping me. Maybe the two of us can help each other out. If you can help me get to my appointment on time tomorrow, I'll have Jason see if he can learn where Fred keeps the picture of you in front of the bank. That is, if you're telling the truth about being innocent."

"I am innocent," Andrew whined. "And I'm also scared to death of your angel. But when push comes to shove, I'm even more scared of Fred. I know what he's capable of, and if he did get that picture into the hands of the authorities, it would ruin my life. If you could give me some proof that your angel could get the picture away from Fred . . ."

"I'll do what I can," Jason said. "Maybe if we're lucky, Fred will let it slip where he keeps the picture. One thing I can do, though. I can have Maggie check the history files in her computer to learn if Andrew is telling the truth about being innocent."

"Jason says he can prove you're innocent, Andrew. And if I get to my interview tomorrow as scheduled, I'll be in a great position to help your cause. Think of all the resources that will be at my disposal once I have my own television talk show. Believe me, Andrew, you're a lot better off helping me out of this mess than you will be going ahead with it."

"I—I don't know. I'll have to think on it some."

"What about Elmo?" Arline asked. "Is Fred blackmailing him, too?"

"No, Uncle Elmo thinks it's all part of a plan cooked up by some guy who wants to fake your kidnapping. He's supposed to show up later and use the fake kidnapping as the perfect time to propose to you."

"Propose to me? You mean like in asking me to marry him?"

"That's the general idea, yes."

"And Elmo fell for a story like that one?"

"You know Fred, Arline. He can be very convincing when he puts his mind to it."

Arline knew Andrew was right. She also knew that Andrew and Elmo both had weaknesses she could work on. Maybe she could find a way to entice one or both of them over to her side. If this were not such a serious problem, she might have found some humor in Fred's story to Elmo. Especially since the man in pursuit on a big motorcycle was indeed planning on proposing marriage, just to someone else.

Feeling the train begin to slow, Arline glanced outside and saw that they were approaching some kind of building. A closer look revealed it was a magnificent old lodge. *How strange,* she thought. *Who would own a lodge up here in these mountains with a personal railroad and all? I'm sure this couldn't be a tourist attraction. I would have heard of it.*

As she looked on in bewilderment, the train circled around the place and came to rest directly in front of it.

"Okay, Arline," Andrew said. "We can get out now."

"This is quite a setup," Jason observed. "I've looked the place over and discovered from old pictures and clippings on the walls it was a tourist lodge several years ago. It's called Henderson's Lodge and obviously has been shut down a long time. Someone's taken pretty good care of it, though. It's in good enough shape to accommodate a group of a hundred or more people right now. And this railroad is pretty elaborate, too. The tracks circle the lodge and then run right back into themselves. The train just makes a loop to let the passengers off, then is set to start back down the mountain on the same tracks that it came up on. One thing about it, Arline. If you had to be kidnapped, this is a pretty nice place for it to happen."

"Oh, thanks a lot, Jason Hackett," Arline muttered sarcastically. "I'll remember that the rest of my life when I think of the great job it cost me."

Andrew shuddered and jumped out of the coach onto the ground ahead of Arline. "I wish you'd stop talking to that angel," he complained. "It's beginning to get on my nerves." Arline laughed at him, and seeing no advantage to remaining in the train, she stepped to the ground herself.

Jason was right about the place. It was not only magnificent, but it looked unbelievably well cared for. Keeping it from the public seemed like such a waste. She vowed that doing a story on this place would be high on her list of priorities once she started her talk show. If she ever started her talk show, that is. Her thoughts became less pleasant as she noticed Fred approaching. Elmo was still in the engine, apparently securing everything.

"I hope you like it here," Fred sneered. "But then you only have to stay a couple of days. Just long enough to miss your interview with Carson. After that, you'll be right here where I can find you when I'm ready to hand you over to the authorities."

"I don't plan on missing that interview, Fred. And in case what little brain you do have between those big ugly ears of yours doesn't realize it, you're in a whole lot of trouble. You and your henchmen here may be spending some time in a less prestigious lodge than this one. I think it's called the Iron Bar Hotel, among other things."

"Get this crazy woman inside, Andy," Fred ordered impatiently. "Maybe when she sees the room I have picked out for her, she'll change her mind about not missing that appointment. It's called the Iron Door Room, among other things."

Andrew began fidgeting nervously. "I—I've been thinking, Fred," he stammered. "What Arline is saying about our being in trouble with the authorities over this thing is true. Kidnapping is a serious offense."

"Come on, Andy. Just how do you think she can ever prove we kidnapped her? It's her word against ours. And when I finish with part two of my plan, nobody will listen to her."

"Yeah, but she has this angel helping her out. I've never gone up against an angel before, and frankly, it scares me pretty bad."

"I was afraid of this," Fred grumbled. "You got to him, didn't you, Miss-High-And-Mighty-Sweet-Talker? Andy is the kind to take your silly story of an angel seriously. Fortunately, I came prepared for just such an emergency." From a holster hidden under the light jacket he was wearing, Fred removed a small caliber automatic pistol and pointed it at the two of them. "You want to be on her side, Andy?" he said. "Then you get can go with her. Get inside, both of you."

Arline didn't move right away. Instead, she glared at Fred. "Now you've included assault with a deadly weapon to your list of crimes. I'm going to enjoy seeing you get what's coming, Fred. And I'm going to dedicate some prime time on my talk show to your fate. Won't that be a stone in your shoe, big man?"

"Don't argue with him, Arline," Jason said. "That's no toy he's holding, and I don't want you hurt. Go along with him for now. We'll figure a way to get you to that interview without getting you shot first."

"I said get inside!" Fred shouted. "Now move it, both of you!"

When she reached the large oak double doors to the lodge, Arline stopped and looked back toward Fred.

"They're not locked," he said. "Open them and go on in." Trying the door on the right, she found he was telling the truth. A very nervous Andrew followed her through the door into a spacious reception area. Fred came in right behind, still holding the weapon.

"Over there," he said, pointing to the reception counter. Arline hesitated just long enough to see where he was pointing.

Once they reached the counter, Fred moved around it and pulled back a large satin drapery, revealing a walk-in bank vault. Gripping the handle to the vault, which was unlocked, he pulled open the heavy door. Arline stared inside at the ten-foot-square room lined with empty shelves.

"You don't really expect me to go in there, do you?" she asked nervously.

"That's the general idea," Fred laughed. "But not until you hand over the keys to your car."

"You're planning on stealing my car, too?"

"Yeah, I've always had this thing for green Toyotas. Let me have those keys."

Arline fished a set of keys from her purse and tossed them to Fred.

"Very good," he said. "Now get in the vault. And just to be sure you don't get lonely, Andy can get in there with you."

"No, please, Fred," Andrew cried. "You know I have claustrophobia. Don't do this to me."

"Shut up and get in the vault. You're the one who wanted to switch over to Arline's side. Now you can have some time to think about what you've done. I'm sure you'll come to your senses before I return from my project back in town."

"How long do you plan on leaving us in there?" Arline asked.

"Not long. As soon as I have time to get a good start down the mountain in old Engine 707, I'll have Uncle Elmo let you out. I do have some heart, you know."

"No, I didn't know," Arline said dryly. "You keep it hidden well."

"You're a fine one to be talking about me not having a heart. I worked hard for the television job, and it rightfully belongs to me. We both know the only reason you were picked is because you're a woman. What we have here is merely a maneuver to put things back the way they belong. Now relax. As soon as I'm on the way down the mountain, you can have the run of the Henderson Lodge for the rest of your stay here. It's really a nice place. I promise you'll enjoy it if you give it a chance. But for now, get in the vault, please."

* * *

Pushing the Kawasaki to its limit, Bruce failed to see the railroad spike pointed sharp side up through a cross tie in the center of the rails. The sound of two blowing tires penetrated his consciousness as he fought to bring the bike safely to a stop.

Bad enough to have blown one tire, Bruce grumbled, *but I managed to get them both.*

Dragging the machine to one side of the tracks, he let it fall to the ground in a useless heap. After taking a moment to clear his head, he made his way further up the mountain on foot. In spite of a good suspension system on the motorcycle, thirty-five miles riding over railroad ties had been a little rough. Some of the time he had been able to travel alongside the tracks, but mostly he had to stay between the rails. At this point, he was so sore even the buttons on his shirt were hurting him.

Rounding a bend in the tracks, he spotted the lodge. Quickly, he crouched behind a large tree on a hill overlooking the area and took stock of the situation below. Somewhere he remembered reading about this place, although he had never seen it before. As he recalled, the owner had died nearly a quarter century ago, leaving the place to his children who chose not to keep it open to the public. It was obvious from the looks of the place that someone had cared for it through the years. He noticed one man standing near the engine of the train, but the others were nowhere in sight.

They must be inside the lodge, he reasoned. Then, as he watched, the door to the lodge opened and a second man stepped out to join the one near the engine. Quickly, but very quietly, Bruce made his way down the hill until he was within hearing distance. Keeping out of sight was easy, thanks to the thick woods surrounding the area. As the men conversed, Bruce strained to hear every word.

"I don't like it one bit, Fred. I'm the only one that's run this here engine in nearly thirty years. Why is it so all-fired important that you take it back down the mountain alone?"

"Relax, Uncle Elmo. I can handle driving this thing okay. You taught me yourself when I was a youngster, remember? I need you here to make sure this little scheme comes off all right. I wanted the make-believe kidnapping to look as real as possible, so I locked Arline and Andy in the walk-in vault behind the counter. You can let them out as soon as I'm a few miles down the track."

"You what?" Elmo sputtered. "Did I hear you say you locked them two in the vault?"

"Yeah, I did. What's the big deal? You can let them out in less than half an hour."

"No I can't, you young fool. I forgot the combination to that lock so many years ago it ain't even funny."

"You forgot the combination?! You must be joking."

"I'm not joking, Fred. I've never closed that vault since the day the boys cleaned it out twenty-five years ago."

"There must be some way to get the vault open."

"Not without a stick of dynamite, there ain't. I'm putting a stop to this crazy little prank of yours right now, boy. You get back in there and stay near that vault to keep them two calm. I'm going down the mountain to get the dynamite. I keep a few sticks stored in the engine house."

"No!" Fred shouted. "I'm the one who's going down the mountain. I'll bring the dynamite with me when I come back. There's too much riding on this to give up now."

"I ain't letting you do it, Fred. It makes no never mind about your fake kidnapping idea. Those two are in big trouble."

"I hate to do this, Uncle Elmo," Fred replied, pulling the automatic pistol out once more. "But we're going to do it my way, and that's that."

"What do you mean, pointing a gun at me, young man? Have you lost all your marbles? That's not a plaything, you know."

"I'm not playing a game here, Uncle. Now get over next to the lodge and lay flat on the ground before I show you just how serious I am about this."

"I don't see why in tarnation it's so blamed important that some fellow go to all this trouble just to propose to that young woman. This younger generation don't make no sense a'tall." Reluctantly, Elmo walked over near the lodge and lay face down on the ground.

"I'll be back," Fred called out as he boarded the engine. "And I'll bring the dynamite with me. I only hope you know how to use it without getting the two of them killed."

"Ha!" Elmo laughed. "You get me one stick of that dynamite,

and I'll blow that door open so easy it won't even raise no dust."

Bruce stayed well hidden until the train pulled away, but wasted no time in getting to Elmo as soon as the coast was clear. "Are you all right, sir?" he asked, helping Elmo to his feet. "I saw the man you called Fred pull a weapon and threaten you."

Elmo brushed the dried grass from his overalls. "Who in tarnation might you be, young fellow?" he asked, looking squint-eyed at Bruce. "Let me guess. You're the one who's planning on proposing to your future wife in the outlandish manner. I'm right, ain't I?"

"Well yes, I suppose you are. But how did you know about that?"

"Never mind how I know for right now. We got ourselves a bigger problem to be dealing with. One question crosses my mind, though. How in blazes did you get up the mountain, anyway?"

"I rode a motorcycle and followed the tracks."

"Well, now, would you look at that? I don't rightly remember it being done that way before. You must be pretty hung up on this gal to go to all this trouble asking her to marry you."

"Yes, sir. I'm in love with her all right. And Arline's doing everything in her power to help me live up to my commitment for the proposal. But if I heard your conversation with Fred correctly, Arline's in big trouble right now."

"That ain't stretching the truth an inch. She and my nephew Andy are in big trouble. Fred's another one of my nephews. He's one that's always been a little on the strange side, but I've never seen him go this far before. If you don't mind my saying so, I think this kidnap plot of yours is pushing things a little too far."

"You're mistaken, sir, if you think I had anything to do with this kidnapping. I witnessed it happen and followed the culprits here to help Arline escape."

Elmo stared at Bruce. "Well, that don't make no sense a'tall. Fred told me—Oh, never mind, let's go inside and see what we can do about those two locked up in the vault."

* * *

As the door to the vault slammed closed with a loud clank, Arline took stock of the situation. At least there was light coming from a single lamp hanging from the ceiling in the center of the room. And there was fresh air coming into the room from a small overhead vent. That was a great relief. Being a big movie buff, she had seen enough plots about people being trapped inside a confined space and running out of oxygen to be glad it couldn't happen in this case. Andrew was hunkered down in one corner of the room, whimpering like a puppy about to be thrown into his bathwater. Jason stood next to her, but even he looked worried.

"You got any ideas how to get me to my interview on time?" she asked sarcastically.

"Not without Gus's help I don't," Jason admitted with a sigh. "At least Bruce is nearby. He made it up the mountain on the Kawasaki. Maybe he can find a way to help."

"If Fred doesn't spot him first," Arline reminded him.

"Is your angel in here with us?" Andrew asked, his eyes bigger than two cotton balls.

"He's here."

"Who's this Bruce fellow you keep mentioning? Is he the boyfriend you've been keeping such tight company with lately?"

"How do you know I've been keeping company with Bruce? Have you and Fred been spying on me?"

Andrew rose to his feet, still looking forlorn. "I told you, Arline. I didn't want anything to do with this whole thing. It was Fred's idea from the beginning. It's just that picture he has of me. You do understand, don't you?"

"I understand the trouble you're in, Andrew. How does Fred plan on getting away with this kidnapping? All I have to do is go to the authorities with the story of what's happened here, and he's busted."

"He plans on discrediting your story by making you look guilty of robbery. He figures to come out looking like a hero by learning of your foul deed and exposing you. He's good at this sort of thing, Arline. And he's planned it out to the smallest detail. I'm telling you, when you accuse him of the kidnapping, it will only come across as an attempt to cover up your own crime."

Arline laughed. "He plans on making me look guilty of robbery? What is it I'm supposed to have stolen?"

"Fred broke into Stewart Carson's private office a couple of weeks back. He stole a valuable gold-plated trophy, and he's going to plant it in your car. That's where he's headed right now. Once he gets the trophy planted, he'll contact Stewart with the story he found you out. He'll take Stewart to your car to let him see the evidence for himself. Next, he'll simply deliver you to the police."

Arline was furious. "How's he planning on getting down from the mountain?" she asked curtly.

"He's taking the train. It's the only way there is to get down the mountain from here. That was a big part of his plan, since it keeps you from interfering until all the loose ends are tied up."

"I'm afraid there's one loose end even Fred failed to think of," Jason interrupted. "I was just checking outside, and I found out some very bad news. It seems that Elmo has forgotten the combination to this vault. Fred's heading down the mountain all right, but there doesn't seem to be a way of getting the two of you out of here until he returns with a stick of dynamite."

"Dynamite?" Arline gasped. "Fred's planning on blasting the vault open? I know you promised I'd go shopping with Sam again someday, but I didn't think you meant this soon. We'll be killed, Jason."

"Elmo seems confident he can blast the door open safely once he has the dynamite. Getting the dynamite is the problem we face right now."

"Oh, isn't this just peachy," Arline said in disgust. "Now what am I supposed to do, send a message to Stewart Carson by carrier pigeon, explaining I can't make my appointment because I'm trapped inside a vault with a crook and an angel?"

"Arline, are you in there? Are you all right?" It was Bruce's voice from outside the vault.

"I'm in here, Bruce. But I'd hardly say I'm all right. Is Elmo with you?"

"He's here with me, but he's forgotten the combination to the lock."

"I know. Jason already told me."

"Is Jason in there with you now?"

"He's here."

"Jason," Bruce cried out. "I've got an idea how we might be able to open this vault, but I need your help."

"Tell him I'll do anything, Arline."

"Jason says he'll do anything you ask, Bruce."

"Good. I'm familiar enough with this kind of lock to know it has three tumblers. By turning the handle first right, then left, then back right again the tumblers will fall in place. That is if I stop on the exact number in each direction when the tumbler is properly lined up to fall in place. That's where you come in, Jason. If you can see inside the lock, you can have Arline tell me when the tumblers are lined up. If you can do that, I'll have this vault open in less than two minutes."

"Yes!" Jason shouted. "I can't believe Bruce came up with this idea, but it will work. Tell him to turn the handle slow enough so I can signal when each tumbler falls into place."

"Jason can do it, Bruce. He says to turn the handle slowly, though."

"Good. Here we go. Tell him to start watching right now."

"He's watching, Bruce," Arline said with a laugh, "and you can't believe how weird he looks with his face buried inside the vault door."

Just as Bruce had promised, the door was open in less than two minutes. At first sight of Bruce, Arline rushed to him, burying herself deep in his large chest. Very slowly, Bruce let his arms slide around her.

"You're trembling," he said softly.

"And you're a mess," she replied with quivering voice. "Are you all right?"

"I managed to fall in a creek," he replied. "And the dust from following Fred's truck sort of stuck to me."

Suddenly, Arline pulled abruptly away and fixed her eyes to his. "I—I'm sorry," she said. "I had no right to do that."

"No, it's quite all right," Bruce quickly assured her. "I'm just glad you're not hurt."

"Ditto," she smiled. "I'm glad you're not hurt, either. That was some stunt you pulled, coming after me on Ted's motorcycle. Jason kept me posted with a mile-by-mile report. It must have been a frightening experience for you."

Bruce rolled his eyes. "That, Arline, is the biggest understatement you've ever come up with. But I couldn't let them hurt you."

"Do you think that motorcycle will get the two of us back down the mountain in time to stop Fred from framing me for robbery?" Arline asked.

"Framing you for robbery? I don't understand."

"I'll explain it to you on the way down, if the motorcycle will get us there."

Bruce winced. "I'm afraid I have some bad news about the motorcycle, Arline. I managed to blow out both tires half a mile back. It's unusable, I'm afraid."

"Are you sure we can't make it work even with the tires blown out?" Arline asked, clinging to one last thread of hope.

"I'm positive."

Arline stood dumbfounded for several seconds. Then, without saying a word, she walked to the large picture window at the front of the reception hall and stared at the mountain scenery outside. A moment later she felt Bruce's hands on her shoulders.

"Well," she sighed in despair. "There goes my dream. It looks like I'll be spending some time being interviewed on television as an accused thief rather than doing the interviewing myself."

"It's all right, darling," Bruce comforted, with a light squeeze on her shoulders. "I feel responsible for getting you into this mess, and I'll find some way to get you out of it, I promise."

Arline spun and stared at Bruce.

"What did you just call me?" she asked in astonishment.

A sudden blush rushed to Bruce's face as he realized what he had said.

"I'm sorry, Arline," he quickly apologized. "I don't know why I used that word. For some reason it just slipped out. It seemed so—natural."

Arline struggled to understand what was happening to her. She used to hate it when Bruce would call Samantha "darling" all the time. But now he had just referred to her by the word. And this time, she didn't mind it. In fact, she even liked the sound of it. It made her feel—sort of—tingly inside.

"It's okay, Bruce," she said. "Hearing you use that word just reminded me of Sam, I suppose."

"Yes. Perhaps I was thinking of Samantha myself. She would have loved it here in these mountains, you know."

"I know, Bruce. She always loved the mountains."

"There is something about this place that appeals to me, as well. I almost wish I could give up my practice and buy it."

"You could, Bruce. I'm sure with a little work you could turn the place into a profitable business."

"Yes, I suppose I could. But," he sighed, "Jenice would never stand for living a peaceful life like this place offers. If I plan to marry her, I can never have thoughts of anything like this."

"I don't understand that woman's attitude," Arline huffed. "If a great guy like you ever proposed to me and offered this kind of life, I'd say yes."

Their eyes met again. "You would?" Bruce asked softly.

"In a heartbeat," she answered.

"Yes, well," Bruce stammered nervously while taking a step backward. "We really should get back to the problem at hand. We must find a way of getting you down this mountain."

"How are you going to do that, Bruce? We have no transportation."

"Well, now, ma'am," Elmo said, approaching from the other side of the room. "That's not exactly true. My fool nephew thinks he's left us up here without transportation, but he's not as smart as he supposes. I still have one way left to get us all down off this mountain—if you don't mind a bit of a bumpy ride, that is."

CHAPTER FOURTEEN

Arline stared at the contraption in front of her and wondered how Elmo expected them to travel the thirty-five miles back to his trailer on whatever it was. And even if by some miracle they did make it that far, what then? How could they ever get back to town in time to stop Fred from carrying out his fiendish plot? Why hadn't she listened to Bruce at the airport? If she hadn't stayed alone at his car while he went to make the call, none of this would have happened.

"What is this thing, Elmo?" she asked dejectedly.

"What is it?" Elmo echoed. "It's Geraldine, that's what it is."

"Geraldine?" Arline looked at Elmo in disbelief.

"Yep. Named her after my wife. She died some thirty years ago." Elmo's eyes grew misty. "Prettiest woman I ever did see and so darn dependable it was spooky. She was the best thing that ever happened to this old codger, I'll tell you for sure. Sure do miss that woman."

Arline watched as Elmo wiped away a tear with the back of his hand. "She sounds wonderful," she said comfortingly.

Elmo sniffed. "This old handcar don't look nothing like her, but it's always been so dependable it just sort of brings her to mind. It just seemed natural to give it her name. Makes me feel close to her whenever I use it."

"But what exactly is it?" Arline asked.

"Putting it in words you can better understand," Elmo explained, "this here's a handcar. The construction crew used to use it to travel the rail line, looking for problems the engineer couldn't see from the big engine. In the old days it was hand-operated by a see-saw handle in the middle. I modernized her a few years back with this old Model A Ford engine. Runs like a top. I rebuilt it myself. We won't have no trouble a'tall getting home with Geraldine here."

Arline and the others watched in amazement as Elmo positioned a few switches and levers. Then, taking a hand crank from a toolbox on the car, he inserted it in one end of the engine and gave a few quick yanks. Nothing happened.

"Are you sure this thing will even run?" Arline asked nervously.

Elmo didn't look at all concerned. "Will the sun come up in the east tomorrow morning?" he asked. "I was only priming some gasoline into the carburetor. Now, if you'll be so kind as to flip that switch right there to the 'up' position, I'll show you how good she runs." Elmo pointed to the switch and Arline turned it on. Gripping the hand crank firmly, he gave one gigantic yank. Suddenly the car began to shake as the four cylinders came to life with a noise that was sweet to Arline's ears.

"It works!" she shouted. "What do we do now?"

"Now," Elmo answered proudly, "we all take a seat and get Geraldine out to the main rail line. That perty red dress of yours ain't the best thing to be wearing for a jaunt like this, but it'll have to do, I reckon."

There were two bench seats, one on each side of the car. Arline sat next to Bruce, while Elmo and Andrew sat opposite them. Elmo pulled a clutch lever and the car jerked into motion. Exiting the building where it had been housed, it bounced along the back section of track toward the switching junction, where the main track could be accessed. Although it had been a nerve-racking day, Arline had to admit she was having fun. Especially since Bruce was next to her.

"There's something I've been meaning to ask," Elmo said, as they moved briskly along. "It's about you, young fellow." He motioned toward Bruce. "I never seen anything like the way you opened that safe back in the lodge. You had some kind of help, didn't you?"

"Yes," Bruce laughed. "I had some help, but it might be a little hard to explain."

"I heard this young woman talks to a ghost. It wouldn't have something to do with that, would it?"

Bruce smiled. "You heard wrong, Elmo. Arline doesn't talk to a ghost at all. She talks to an angel. A very special angel, who I hope I can refer to as my friend."

Arline could hardly believe what she was hearing, and she glanced around to catch Jason's reaction, only to discover he was nowhere to be seen.

"I wonder where he disappeared to so suddenly?" she mused. Then, noticing the puzzled looks on all three men's faces, she added, "Jason, I mean. He's just vanished."

"Perhaps he's checking on our friend Fred," Bruce suggested.

Arline nodded. "You're probably right, Bruce. At a time like this, I'm glad to have that crazy angel on my side."

"So am I," Bruce agreed. "So am I."

The trip down the hill took only a half hour or so longer than it would have taken in the train. This was mainly because it was all downhill, and they were able to coast much faster than the little four-cylinder engine could have taken them. As Elmo had predicted, it was a bumpy ride, but not at all unpleasant. Once, when they were about halfway down the hill, Arline was surprised to feel Bruce slip his hand into hers. She said nothing, nor did she pull away. And regardless of how hard she tried, she couldn't shake the feeling of liking his hand there. After a few minutes, Bruce became aware of what he had done and quickly removed his hand.

The first indication they were nearing their destination was the sound of old Rastus's barking. Then, just as they were rounding the last turn, bringing the red building in sight, Jason returned.

"Well," Arline said to him. "You were gone long enough. Where have you been? Checking up on old Fred, I hope."

"Jason's back?" Bruce asked.

"He is."

"I was checking on Fred all right, but that's not the only place I've been. The reason I took so long is because I stopped in to see Maggie and had her locate Geraldine Spatford for me."

"Geraldine Spatford?" Arline asked.

"Yeah, Elmo's wife."

"What about Geraldine Spatford?" Elmo asked, looking squint-eyed at Arline. "And how did you know my last name?"

"Jason told me."

"Jason? You mean that angel fellow you talk to?"

"In the flesh—uh . . . well not exactly, but you know what I mean."

"I talked with Geraldine," Jason continued. "She wants me to send her love to Elmo. She says she misses him terribly and promises to be there to meet him when it comes his time."

"Jason tells me he talked to your Geraldine, Elmo. She misses you very, very much and wants you to know when the time comes for you to join her, she'll be the one who's there to meet you."

Elmo looked delighted. "Your angel talked to Geraldine? You mean to tell me I really will get to see her again someday?"

"You bet he will," Jason assured. "And if the two of them are as much in love as they seem, things can be worked out so they never have to be apart again." It took Arline nearly half a minute to get control over her voice in order to relay Jason's message to Elmo. Even then, she was so choked up it was hard to get out.

"I can be with Geraldine again? Them's the best sounding words I've ever heard in my life."

"And," Jason added, "she's planning on fixing your favorite dinner when you get there. Roast jackrabbit."

"Are you kidding me?" Arline asked Elmo. "Is roast jackrabbit your favorite meal?"

"Yes, by splendors it is. Did Geraldine tell your angel that, too?"

"She did, and you get it for your first meal after she picks you up."

"There is one thing I wouldn't tell him, Arline," Jason said with a smile. "She plans on making him pay for naming that handcar after her."

Arline winked her agreement and said nothing.

It was a happy Elmo who brought the handcar to a stop just behind the train that Fred had left deserted before leaving for town in his pickup truck.

"By jingles," he said, killing the little engine, "I reckon you folks will be needing some transportation into the city now, won't you?"

"To be sure," Bruce quickly answered. "Would you be able to help us out in that department?"

"Course I can. I keep old Henry under a tarp on the far side of my trailer. Come on, I'll get the old fellow out for you."

Elmo led the way to the vehicle where, with the help of Bruce and Andrew, he removed the tarp.

"Wow!" Bruce cried at first sight of the truck. "What on earth kind of a truck is this?"

Elmo laughed. "It's a 1932 Ford. Sure is a beauty, ain't it?"

"Well, yes, I suppose so. I've certainly never seen anything like it before."

"Take a look at this engine," Elmo beamed, lifting one section of the side mount hood. "It's one of the first V-8s ever to be put in production. So far as I'm concerned, these old flathead engines are way out in front of the complicated junk they put in cars these days."

"I'll take your word for it," Bruce shrugged. "I'm not very mechanically inclined, you see."

Elmo moved to the door on the driver's side, which, unlike modern cars, opened from the front to the back.

"You're not one of them fellows that's never driven a stick shift with a foot clutch, are you?" he asked.

"Well I—"

"I can drive the car," Arline broke in. "I'm sure it's not that much different from any other manual shift, and I've driven plenty of those."

Bruce objected. "I'm sure you could do a much better job driving the car than I can, Arline. But I'd like to give this a try. How hard can it be after the trip up the hill I just mastered?"

"All right, Bruce, if that's what you want. I hope you can get the hang of it in a hurry, though. Fred has a pretty healthy head start on us, you know."

After Jason explained what he had found while checking on Fred earlier, Arline said to Bruce, "Jason says Fred is on his way to my place. We'd better get started."

Elmo handed Bruce the keys to the Ford. "Don't worry about the truck, young man. It's only a thing. If something gets broke, I can either fix it or replace it. If push comes to shove I can do without it. It don't make no never mind to me, just as long as you catch that nephew of mine before he messes up your girlfriend's life. I hate to say it, but he's one that should be pulled off the streets and put away for good. My grandaddy would be ashamed to have anyone know Fred sprang from our family tree."

Arline got in on the driver's side and scooted across. It was a bit of a tight fit getting past the floor shift, but she made it okay. Bruce climbed behind the wheel and gave the controls a thorough once-over.

"Thanks, Elmo," he said, closing the door. "You're a good man, and I promise to see to it you're paid back for this favor. How do you start this thing, anyway?"

Elmo pointed to a foot lever mounted on the floor near the brake pedal. Bruce turned on the key. Then, with his left foot on the clutch, he pressed the lever with his right foot. The starter ground a few seconds and the old V-8 came to life. Andrew leaned against Arline's side of the car. "Please," he begged, "See if your angel can do something about that picture. I'll do anything you ask of me, if you can only get that picture away from Fred."

"I'll do what I can, Andrew. I give you my word," Arline promised.

At that moment, Bruce let out the clutch and the old Ford lurched forward in a series of wild jolts. Andrew dove for cover on one side of the truck, while Elmo did the same on the opposite side. Even Rastus ran for the woods, tail between his legs. Before Bruce and Arline had finished traveling the ten miles of dirt trail to Highline Road, Bruce had pretty much figured out how to handle the truck.

Suddenly Jason appeared in the car with them. "You had better hurry," he warned. "Fred is just now pulling up to your driveway."

* * *

An evil smile crossed Fred's lips as he found Arline's Toyota parked in front of her house, just as he had expected. Slipping on a pair of gloves, he reached behind the seat and removed a large metal box. Laying it on the seat next to him, he unlocked and opened it. Next, he removed two objects. One was the expensive trophy he had stolen from Stewart Carson's office, the other a five-by-seven picture of Cousin Andrew sitting at the wheel of his car in front of the bank. After looking the picture over for a minute, Fred returned it to the box, which he locked once again and placed back behind the seat. Taking the trophy with him, he crossed the driveway to Arline's car.

After digging her keys from his pocket, he unlocked the door and lay the trophy in plain sight on the front seat.

"That ought to do it," he sneered, closing and relocking the door. "When old Carson sees that, Arline's television career is over. And mine is in the bag. Let's see if her make-believe angel can help her out of this one."

"Make-believe, am I?" Jason huffed. "We'll see about that, Freddy old boy. I'd say you're in for the shock of your life."

Jason watched as Fred removed the gloves, got back in his truck, and pulled a sheet of scrap paper from the glove compartment. Straining to see what was written on the paper, Jason read, "1205 Smoketree Lane."

"Is that where we're going next, Fred?" he asked. Sure enough, Fred pulled away from Arline's place and headed in the direction of Smoketree Lane.

"Okay," Jason said. "I'll just run on ahead and see who lives there. I'm sure when I learn who it is, I'll know more about what you're up to, little man."

CHAPTER FIFTEEN

The sun was just sinking out of sight on a very long day as Jason stood in front of the elegant home on Smoketree Lane, reading the name on the large brass door plaque. *Stewart Carson? I don't believe it. Fred is going straight to Stewart Carson with the story he found the trophy in Arline's car. How brazen can one man get? I'm going to enjoy seeing this guy get what he has coming.*

Jason was about to go back to Arline with what he had just learned when a familiar voice caught his attention. "I'm glad ta see yer still on the job, pal. I was beginnin' ta worry what I might find when I got back, but it looks like you have things pretty much under control."

"Gus? I never thought I'd be this glad to see you. I hope your conference was worth it. I sure could have used your help here a few times the last three weeks."

"I got back just as soon as I could, Jason. I still can't figure why so many things are goin' wrong on this project. Somehow the message for me to attend the conference got on my computer by mistake. I should never have been invited in the first place."

"What?! You mean you deserted me all this time for nothing? If you weren't supposed to be at the conference, why the heck didn't you get back here where you were needed? For crying out loud, Gus. This is your project, you know."

"Take it easy, Jase, it's not my fault. Once I got there, the higher authorities decided I should stick around. They said it would be a good learnin' experience for me. I gotta admit it was pretty interestin'. If I hadn't been so nervous about what was goin' on back at the home front, I could have enjoyed it. I never saw anythin' like it before. They were puttin' together the final plans for creatin' another world like this one. I even got ta meet my future counterpart."

"You met their Special Contracts Coordinator?"

"Yep. A real nice fella, too. He talks sorta funny, though."

"I hope you advised him to wait until his secretary is there to type his contracts instead of trying to do it himself."

"You got a mean streak a mile wide, pal. Aren't ya ever gonna let me forget about that typo?"

"Not in this eternity, I'm not. Are you through chasing about the universe long enough to help me finish up this project? I only have one day left to get Bruce ready to jump out of that airplane, you know."

"I gotta spend tomorrow reportin' back ta my Area Supervisor on the conference, but I'll be there when Bruce is ready ta make the jump. If necessary, I'll give him a push myself. For now, you get back and warn Arline what old Fred's up to. We can't just leave her hangin' after all she's done for us."

"You mean you're not even going to help me out with Fred Goodson's little ploy? I'd think you could at least do that much."

"My hands are tied, Jason. I gotta spend tonight gettin' my notes together for my report tomorrow. Yer doin' great without me. Just hang in there one more day."

For well over a minute after Gus left, Jason stood alone, pondering and fuming over the events of the last month. *How do I get myself into these situations?* he mused. At last he shrugged and returned to Bruce and Arline, who were just a few blocks from her place.

"I've got some bad news, and some bad news," he said, without the slightest hint of encouragement in his demeanor. "Which do you want to hear first?"

Arline grimaced. "You're just full of good cheer. Dare I ask what's going on now?"

"I'll start with the bad news. Fred's planted the trophy in your car and he's on his way to Stewart Carson's house right now. I can only assume he's going there with the idea of framing you for stealing it."

In disgust, Arline slammed her right foot against the floorboard of the old truck. The force of her foot striking the bare metal tore loose the heel from her shoe and left it dangling uselessly by a bit of leather.

"Wouldn't you know it!" she fumed. "As if things weren't bad enough, now I go and break off the heel of my shoe. You said there was more bad news. You might as well tell me the rest of it. I still have one heel left to tear off."

"The rest of my news concerns Gus. He made it back from his little jaunt across the skies. I talked to him not five minutes ago."

"That's not bad news, Jason. Maybe Gus can use some of the trickery you tell me he's so good at to help us."

"That's what I was hoping for, too, Arline. But as fate would have it, he's up to his ears in notes that he has to get together for a report to the higher authorities. He has an appointment tomorrow morning and has to account for his time at the conference. He'll be of no help to us tonight, I'm sorry to say."

"What is Jason saying?" Bruce asked anxiously. "Has he learned what Fred's up to?"

"I'm afraid he has, Bruce. And it doesn't look good for me, unless we can move fast enough to foil his little scheme. Jason tells me Fred's planted the stolen trophy in my car and is now on his way to Stewart Carson's house. You know what that means."

"Fred intends on pinning the theft on you. One thing I don't understand, however. How did Fred manage to get the trophy into your car? You do keep it locked, I assume."

"I had the car locked, but Fred took my keys from me back at the lodge."

"This could be serious. If Fred has your keys it will make it difficult for us to get the car open to remove the trophy. I have a friend who is a locksmith, but we have so little time."

Arline removed her shoe and pulled the dangling heel the rest of the way off. "Drat," she said. "These were the only pair of red heels I own. Don't worry about getting into my car. I keep a spare set of keys hidden in a little box under the back bumper."

"At least something is going our way," Bruce said with a sigh. "We have to get that trophy out of your car fast."

"We have to do that, all right," Arline agreed. "But I think we should carry it a step further. I think we should turn Fred's little game around on him."

"You mean . . . ?"

"I mean we plant the trophy in Fred's truck. Then we can figure some way of leading Stewart to it."

"That's a great idea, Arline. But it will require some split-second timing. I'm pushing this old truck as fast as it will go now."

"You're doing great," Arline encouraged. "I can't believe how well you've adjusted to driving a standard shift. Are you sure this is your first time?"

"Yes," he laughed. "It's my first time. It seems I've had a lot of 'firsts' lately. I'm not sure this is the best time to bring it up, but you've been good for me, Arline. I want you to know how grateful I am for what you've done. I'm still not sure I can jump out of that plane tomorrow, but if I do go through with it, you get all the credit. If things work out like they're supposed to, I'm sure Jenice will want to thank you as well."

Angry as she was at Fred, Bruce's remarks about Jenice brought another feeling to her. It was a feeling she didn't understand, nor could she describe it. She forced the thoughts from her mind and returned to the problem at hand.

Bruce pulled the old truck to a stop in front of her house and turned off the noisy engine.

"Let's get to work," he said, climbing out of the truck and moving quickly to the green Toyota parked in the driveway. Arline got out and followed him. By the time she got to her car, Bruce had already located the hidden keys and had the door unlocked. Sure enough, the trophy was lying on the seat, just as Jason had said.

"I think we can make better time in your Toyota than we can in the old Ford," Bruce suggested. "What do you say we use it to get us to Stewart's place?"

"Sounds good to me," Arline agreed. "Let's do it."

As she backed the car out of the driveway, it was Jason's turn to come up with a suggestion. "If you take the freeway to Summerview Drive, then head back north to Smoketree Lane, you can cut twenty minutes off the time it takes to get to Stewart's place," he said.

"I don't think so," Arline argued. "It would be several miles further that way. I'm sure it will be faster to take the back roads to his place."

"Listen to me, Arline. I know what I'm talking about. The twenty years I spent waiting for Sam to grow up, I had to find some pretty strange things to occupy my time. I did a lot of people-watching. That often meant riding around in the car with some interesting souls. I learned just about everything there is to know about the roads around here. I'm telling you, my way will save you twenty minutes at least."

Arline paused to consider a moment. "Okay, Jason, the freeway it is," she said. "You've never been wrong yet."

* * *

Switching off his engine, Fred looked at Stewart Carson's home and gathered his thoughts together. He had to be careful with this part of his plan. Convincing Stewart he had proof of Arline's guilt in the robbery would require the best performance of his life. The hardest part would be enticing Stewart into going with him to Arline's place to see the evidence firsthand. He had always thought of himself as a man with a golden tongue. Now would be his greatest hour of proof.

Pulling together his courage, Fred opened the truck door and stepped out onto the sidewalk. A moment later he stood at the front door, staring at the little brass switch. Here goes, he thought, placing his finger on the switch and giving a quick push. The door chimes sounded, and after what seemed like an incredibly long time, the door opened and Fred was face-to-face with Stewart Carson for the first time since being fired.

"Fred Goodson?" Stewart asked gruffly. "What are you doing here?"

"Please, Mr. Carson, just let me have a minute of your time. I think what I have to say will be of interest to you, if you'll only hear me out."

"What could you possibly have to say to me that I would find interesting?"

"It's about your stolen trophy, sir. The one taken when your office was broken into a few weeks ago."

"What do you know about my trophy?" Stewart asked, his interest immediately picking up.

"I read about the robbery in the paper. I had my suspicions at the time about who must have taken it, and why. I did some investigating, and I was right. I not only know who stole your trophy, I know where it is at this very moment." Staring into the cold hard eyes of Stewart Carson, Fred nervously shifted his weight from one leg to the other and went on with his lie. "If I could only have a few minutes of your time, I'll explain everything."

Stewart's eyes narrowed, and his normally deep voice became even deeper. "Why would you take time to investigate the theft of my trophy? It couldn't be out of the goodness of your heart. Not after I fired you."

"I was hoping, sir, that if you appreciate my efforts in helping return your trophy, you might consider giving me back my job."

After thinking over what Fred was saying, Stewart stepped aside, making room for him to enter the house.

"By all means," he said, "Step inside and we'll talk."

After being led to Stewart's living room and declining the offer to sit down, Fred continued to spin his concocted story. "You might remember, sir," he said in his most persuasive voice, "I threatened Arline with trouble the day of the contest. I should never have done it, but I was hurt and angry at the time. I freely admit now, the way I went about trying to win that contest was wrong and foolish. My threats to Arline meant nothing, and I would have dropped the matter altogether if it hadn't been for a phone call from her the day after your office was burglarized. Not that Arline confessed to me or anything. She only let me know that steps had been taken to ensure I could never return to favor in your eyes, sir. Well, after reading about the stolen trophy, I began putting little things together and came to the conclusion she figured you'd blame me for the theft. I've been keeping an eye on her ever since. Tonight it paid off. I've found the trophy, sir. It's in her Toyota, which I saw parked in her driveway not more than forty-five minutes ago."

Stewart looked at Fred suspiciously. "You saw my trophy in Arline's car? Why didn't you call the police?"

"I didn't call the police for two reasons, sir. First, I thought you might like to handle the problem yourself. I know you've taken a liking to Arline, and I wasn't sure you'd want to have her arrested.

Second, I was hoping to gain favor with you, as I've already explained. I'd like to ask you to come with me back to Arline's place, where you can see the evidence for yourself."

Stewart balked. "You want me to go to Arline's place? How do I know the car is still there? You said it's been nearly an hour since you saw it."

"She's on a date, sir. I assure you the car will be there with the trophy still in it for you to see, if you'll only come with me now."

Stewart moved to a table near the end of his large white leather couch and picked up a picture taken at the time of the presentation of the trophy. He studied the picture for a few minutes, then asked, "Why would Arline leave the trophy in her car, Fred? Wouldn't that be rather foolish on her part?"

Fred had already prepared his answer. "You know how these criminal types are, Mr. Carson. They think of themselves as clever, when in actuality they're usually very stupid. She probably thinks no one would ever suspect her enough to check out her car."

"Perhaps," Stewart said softly. "In any case, it's worth checking out. I'll go with you, Fred, but this had better not be a waste of my time."

"Oh, no, sir," Fred hastily answered, the corners of his mouth curling into a grin. "I'm sure it won't be a waste of your time at all."

* * *

"You'd better hurry," Jason urged as Arline pulled to a stop in the shadows across the street from Stewart Carson's home. "The two of them will be coming out of the house any time now. Fred has convinced Stewart the trophy is in your car, and he's about to take Stewart back to your place."

"Stewart and Fred could be coming out of the house any second," Arline repeated for Bruce's sake. "Jason tells me that Fred plans on taking Stewart to my house."

"I think it's about time we give Fred a little surprise," Bruce said, grabbing the trophy and wiping it clean with his handkerchief. "You wait here. I'll be right back." Arline watched anxiously as Bruce darted across the street, carrying the trophy with his handkerchief. Upon reaching the pickup truck, he tossed the trophy to the front seat through an open window. Then, instead of returning immediately to her car, he knelt down next to the front tire.

"Tell him to get out of there!" Jason shouted. "They're on their way to the front door right now."

"Bruce!" she called out quickly. "You're out of time! Get back here fast!"

A moment later, Bruce was on a dead run toward the Toyota. Just as he dove inside and slammed the door, Fred and Stewart emerged from the house.

"It's too late for me to drive away," Arline said. "Do you suppose they'll notice us here?"

"I don't think so," Bruce answered between gasps for breath. "It's pretty dark. Just keep your head down and don't make any noise."

"What were you doing over there, anyway? You might have been seen."

Bruce held out his hand for Arline to see his small pocketknife and the stem off Fred's front tire. "I've been carrying this knife in my pocket ever since the fishing trip with my father," he answered softly. "It reminds me of a side of him I've only just discovered."

"You flattened Fred's tire with it?"

"We don't want him making a quick getaway, do we?" Bruce pointed out. "Besides, he got two of mine earlier this morning. As the old saying goes, what goes around comes around. Now if I only had my briefcase, I could use my cellular phone to call the police. Unfortunately, it's at home on my bed."

Jason spoke up. "If his briefcase is at home on his bed, then what's this one doing here on the backseat with his name on it?"

"What?" Arline asked, turning around to see what Jason was referring to. "Well, I'll be. There is a briefcase back there, and it looks like yours, Bruce."

"That's impossible," Bruce exclaimed, retrieving the case and looking it over. "It does seem to be mine, though." Quickly, he punched in the combination and flipped the latch. To his amazement, it opened. There inside were all his papers and his cellular telephone, just as he had left it the last time it was used. "I don't understand. Jason must have brought it here somehow?"

Jason quickly disagreed. "He's wrong, Arline. I'm as much in the dark how it got here as the two of you. My guess would be Gus. He might have moved it to your car before he left to prepare his report."

"No matter how it got here, I'm just glad it's here," Arline said thankfully. "Why don't you make that call to the police, Bruce?"

Fred reached for the pickup door and pulled it open as Stewart rounded the truck to get in on the opposite side. Suddenly, he spotted the trophy.

"No!" he screamed. "How . . . ? Wait, Mr. Carson, don't open that—"

It was too late. Stewart had already opened the door and was looking straight at the trophy that was lying in plain sight.

"What's going on here, Fred?" he demanded loudly.

"I can explain," Fred groped, as sweat began showing on his brow.

"You can do your explaining to the police, young man. I'll just take this trophy along with me as evidence."

Picking up the trophy, Stewart started back toward the house, when Fred stepped directly in his path. "No, don't call the police! Let me explain first."

"Get out of my way, Fred. I'm not interested in hearing anything you have to say at this point."

"It was my cousin Andrew!" Fred cried out. "Yes, that's it! My cousin Andrew broke into your office and took the trophy. I was merely returning it to you. I have proof Andy is a crook. I keep the proof in a box behind the seat of my pickup."

Stewart's face showed his disgust. "You can't seem to make up your mind who to lay the blame on can you, Fred? If you ask me, I'd say you've slipped a cog or two off-center. Now get out of my way."

"It's all right," Bruce said, as he stepped from the shadows into full view of the two men. "I've already called the police. They're on their way here this very moment."

"Arline?!" Fred shrieked, as she stepped up to join Bruce, who was crossing the street toward him. "This can't be! How did you—"

"Escape your little trap?" she asked, finishing Fred's sentence for him. "I have an angel, remember. You can't fight an angel, Fred. You'll lose every time."

Breaking for the truck, Fred leapt inside and started the engine. Before he had gone ten feet, he realized the flattened tire made it undrivable. Eyes filled with terror, he jumped out and broke into a run across a neighboring lawn. It took less than twenty steps for Bruce to catch up with him and bring Fred hard to the ground with a flying tackle that would have brought fear to the heart of Joe Montana on his best day in the NFL.

"Way to go!" Jason shouted. "I'm really beginning to like you, Bruce. You're not such a wimp after all." Then he added, more softly, "But it took Arline to prove it to both of us."

Bruce had little trouble convincing Fred to rejoin the others, and as they approached, Arline gave Fred a piercing look.

"There's one other thing I should have mentioned, Fred," she said. "Bruce, here, is on my side, too. It looks like you're completely outnumbered, old friend."

"What's going on here, Arline?" Stewart asked sharply. "Has Fred completely lost his sanity?"

"It would seem so, wouldn't it?" Arline was happy to explain. "It was his intention to convince you that I was the one who broke into your office and stole the trophy. He figured that would get me out of the picture and leave the television position open for grabs. With him being the one to supposedly solve the robbery, he assumed you'd give him another shot at the job."

"Why am I not surprised?" Steward snorted. "I must have been having a relapse of my old malaria problem to have ever considered you for the position in the first place, Fred. I'll tell you this much, you'll never work in the media industry again. Not as long as I'm alive."

At that moment a patrol car turned the corner and pulled into Stewart's driveway. A police officer stepped out of the car and walked slowly toward the group.

"Say, don't I know you?" he asked, looking at Bruce.

"Hello, Officer Brady," Bruce answered. "You made out the report when my house was broken into a little over a year ago."

"Yeah, I remember now," Officer Brady said, scratching the back of his head. "You're the one with the psychic girlfriend who helped us catch those crooks at Silvester's Packing House. They turned out to be a couple of guys we'd been after for a long time. They won't be breaking into any houses for a long time to come. We put them away so deep, they'll be old men before they see this side of the prison wall again." Officer Brady glanced toward Arline. "Is this the lady with the psychic powers by any chance?" he asked.

Although Jason had been the one to find the robber's hideout, Bruce had claimed Samantha was psychic, because that was easier to explain.

"No, officer." He shook his head. "This is Arline Wilson. However—" he smiled and glanced toward Arline "—she does have the same psychic powers as Samantha, the woman you remember from last time."

"I see," Brady said, although his expression was skeptical. Shoving his hat back on his head, he asked, "What seems to be the problem this time?"

Bruce explained. "The trophy Mr. Carson is holding was stolen by someone who broke into his office a couple of weeks back. We found it in this man's pickup truck. I managed to grab him as he was trying to escape. I'd be careful if I were you, officer. He has a gun in his inside coat pocket."

"A gun, you say?" Brady asked wryly. With a big arm around Fred's neck and a night stick hard against his back, Officer Brady took custody from Bruce. In one swift movement, he had Fred spread-eagle against the side of the pickup. Sure enough, a quick but thorough body search turned up the pistol.

"Do you have a permit to carry this?" Brady asked as he removed the clip and checked the chamber to be sure it was empty.

"No, sir," Fred explained, desperately. "I have the gun to protect myself from my cousin Andrew. He's the one who broke into Stewart's office and stole the trophy. Andy has a terrible temper, and I was afraid what might happen to me when he learned I had turned him in. If you'll look behind the seat of my pickup, you'll find a locked metal box. Inside the box is something I'm positive you'll be interested in seeing."

Moving Fred's hands behind his back, Officer Brady slid on a pair of handcuffs and snapped them closed. Next he forced Fred to the ground, where he had him lay facedown on the soft lawn. Only then did he ask, "So what's in the box that you think I might be so interested in?"

Arline wanted to say something in defense of Andrew. But just as she opened her mouth, Jason stopped her. "Let it go, Arline. I'm not sure what's going on here, but Maggie just sent word to me telling me it's been taken care of."

"Do you suppose Maggie found out Andrew is actually guilty?" Arline whispered, so only Jason could hear.

"I'm not sure. All I know is she wants us to let it go."

"Do you remember the bank robbery a little over a year ago?" Fred asked. "The one where you caught two of the thieves, but the driver of the getaway car got away?"

After a moment's thought, Officer Brady replied, "I remember. The guy drove a blue Ford Escort, and we never found him."

"The key to the box is with my other keys in the ignition of the pickup," Fred said eagerly. "Get the box and open it up. Once you see the picture I have there, you'll know who drove the car. Then you'll know I'm telling the truth about who stole the trophy, as well."

Keeping one eye on Fred, Brady retrieved the box and keys from the ignition. Laying the box on the edge of the truck bed, he unlocked and opened it. Everyone watched with keen interest as he removed a five-by-seven photo and looked it over carefully.

"If I remember right, Mr. Vincent," Brady said after studying the picture several seconds, "you're a psychologist, aren't you?"

"Yes, officer. I'm a psychologist. Why?"

"I think this guy is in serious need of your services. I'm afraid you'll have to make his appointments in a jail cell instead of at your office, though. Here, look at this." The officer handed Bruce the picture he had been looking at. Arline and Jason strained to see it over his shoulder.

It was a picture taken in front of the bank, all right. And the two convicted robbers were in the car, dressed as they were at the time of their arrest. The only thing different from the way Fred had described the picture was the driver of the car. It wasn't Andrew at the wheel; it was Fred Goodson.

"I don't understand," Jason commented. "I saw the picture before, and Andrew was sitting where Fred is pictured now. Gus must have taken the picture to Maggie to have it altered by her computer."

At the moment, Arline didn't care how the picture had been altered. Her only thought was that Fred deserved what he was about to receive, regardless how it came about. She watched in amusement as Officer Brady put the photograph, metal box, and automatic pistol in the front seat of his patrol car, then returned to the group.

"I'll need to take the trophy you're holding with me, sir," he said to Stewart. "It's evidence, you know."

"I understand, officer," Stewart replied as he surrendered the trophy to Brady.

"What are you doing? Doesn't that picture mean anything at all to you?" Fred demanded as Officer Brady escorted him to the patrol car and put him into the backseat.

"Oh, yes, it does. It means a great deal. Now, if you'll be so kind as to let me read you your rights, we can get on with this little game of yours."

CHAPTER SIXTEEN

To a passerby, the two people facing each other on Arline's front porch late that night would have offered an amusing sight. The new red dress Arline had chosen to wear that morning was not so lovely now. There was a tear in one sleeve, a few oil spots from a railway handcar, and more wrinkles than if it had lain a week at the bottom of her clothes hamper. Not that the dress was the only thing distracting about Arline's appearance. Her hair looked as if she had just come through a hurricane, and the missing heel from one shoe left her standing lopsided.

Bruce didn't look much better himself. For a man who normally kept every hair in place and would never leave a trace of dirt beneath a fingernail, he definitely looked out of character. Covered every inch with caked dirt from his motorcycle ride, he looked more like a mud wrestler than a polished, competent psychologist. Still, as Arline gazed tenderly into his dark eyes, she knew she was seeing a Bruce she had never known before. Less than a month ago she had dedicated herself into turning him into the man she saw now, but somehow the pleasure of success didn't taste as sweet as it should have. A few more minutes, and they would say goodnight. After that, their lives would drift back into the routine of pursuing their own separate destinies.

Tomorrow, Arline would meet with Stewart Carson to finalize her new television show. Then, on the following day, Bruce would leap from the sky into the waiting life of Jenice Anderson. A leap that would take him forever away from Arline Wilson.

At that moment, her melancholy thoughts were interrupted by the sound of Bruce's question.

"Is Jason still here?" Bruce asked.

"Uh—no," she answered, surprised at the quiver in her usually even voice. "Jason left right after Fred's arrest. He told me he has a very big date with Sam tonight. The two of them are attending what he compared to one of our Easter Pageants. He said he was limited as to what he could tell me about it, but explained that it's a very special event over there. Especially since the main character is played by Himself."

"I see," Bruce replied. "That would be a special event, wouldn't it?" Then, without warning, he gently touched Arline's face. "I'm glad Jason is not around for once," he whispered.

Feeling the warmth of his hand, Arline's heart began pounding so loudly that she was afraid Bruce would hear it.

"What do you mean?" she asked.

"I mean I—I just want to thank you for all you've done for me. I don't know what I would have done without your help."

"Oh." Arline didn't know what to say.

"There is one more thing I'd like to ask of you, though. If you don't mind, that is."

"No!" she quickly responded. "You can ask anything. Anything at all."

"This is a little embarrassing for me to admit, but you see, I've never felt at ease kissing a woman. Not even Samantha, I'm sorry to say. I'm just not the romantic type when it comes to expressing my love. I was wondering . . ."

"If I could give you some pointers?" Arline asked dryly.

"Something like that, I suppose."

"If you'd like to kiss me, it's all right. I mean, we both know you'd just be pretending I'm Jenice and all—wouldn't we?"

"Yes, of course, that's what we'd be doing," Bruce said quickly. "It would just be to help me improve my technique."

Like two statues, they stood for a long moment gazing into each other's eyes. At last, Bruce slid his arm around Arline and pulled her slowly to him. Their lips barely touched. Molding herself into his embrace, Arline's arms came to rest on his shoulders, and she marveled at how broad and strong they felt. He pulled her into a deeper kiss, one that left her warm and secure. She wished this moment could last forever. After what seemed a hundred heartbeats, their lips parted.

"How was it?" Bruce asked softly.

"I'm not sure," Arline whispered. "Maybe if we try again?" This time it was Arline who kissed Bruce. The second kiss lasted longer than the first. Then, after a lingering sigh, she forced herself to say, "Jenice is a very lucky woman. I can't remember when I've been kissed like that, Bruce. There's nothing I can think of to help you improve your technique."

"Thank you," he answered with a sigh of his own. "You'll never know how grateful I am for all you've done for me."

Arline looked at his face for a long moment. "I hesitate to mention this, Bruce, but your left eye is twitching," she said. "I've noticed it often does that when something's on your mind."

"Oh, yes," Bruce said, quickly moving a hand to cover his eye. "It's a nervous disorder I've had since I was a child. It's a little embarrassing at times."

"There's nothing to be embarrassed about. I was just wondering what was on your mind to cause the twitching now?"

"I—I'm really not sure. Perhaps it's from realizing how close I am to the time I must make one of the most difficult decisions of my life."

"Stepping out of an airplane at three thousand feet over Howard Placard's private beach?"

"Yes."

"Do you think you'll be able to do it?"

"I'm still not sure. If I can do it, it's only because of you. I don't suppose you'd consider being in the plane with me when I have to make the decision, would you?"

"No, Bruce. I've done all I can do to help you. It wouldn't be right for me to be there. That moment belongs to you and Jenice."

"Yes," Bruce said, with another heavy sigh. "I'm sure you're right." He took a deep breath and exhaled slowly. "I suppose I'd better be going now. After the day we've just put in, we both could use some sleep."

Never had any words come with such disappointing force to Arline's heart. She wished with every ounce of her soul she could reach out and hold onto Bruce so tightly he couldn't walk out of her life. But she knew that was not possible. Bruce belonged to another, and refusing to let him go was not an option.

"Yes," she answered, fighting to hold back the tears. "I guess it is time we say our good-byes. I want you to know I think you're a very special man, Bruce. I wish you and Jenice all the happiness in the world."

"And I think you're very special, Arline. Best of luck in your new job. You'll do wonderfully, I'm sure. I'll always be your biggest fan. And thanks for allowing me to use your car to get home tonight. I'll have the auto club return it with a full tank of gasoline first thing in the morning."

Had this been a scene from some romantic movie, this is where the soft music would have begun. As if in big-screen slow motion, Arline watched Bruce walk to her car. Once inside he gave one last wave and then drove away. She continued to watch long after the Toyota was out of sight. Then, with a heavy heart, she stepped inside and closed the door. What little sleep she did manage that night was restless and anything but relaxing.

* * *

As the sun rose on the long-anticipated day of her appointment with Stewart Carson, Arline struggled with her feelings. *What is the matter with you, Arline Wilson?* she asked herself. *This should be the most exciting day of your life, and all you can think of is Bruce Vincent. This is crazy. Get hold of yourself, woman. Put your priorities back where they belong, and start thinking of your great new future instead of the passing fun you've shared with Bruce the last few weeks.*

It was useless. Thoughts of Bruce refused to go away. Again and again she relived those special moments they had spent together. She ran barefoot with him on the soft, sandy beach. She laughed with him as they watched their kite fly majestically over the white-capped ocean. A smile crossed her lips as she remembered his face when he caught his first fish. And best of all, she remembered last night's kiss.

Stepping outside for the morning paper, she was taken aback to find her car already returned. In the front seat were a dozen red roses. Holding them close to her heart, she breathed deeply of the sweet aroma and wished they had been given for a different reason. Lovely as they were, they only told her Bruce was gone forever. Fighting back the pain, she set about the task of going on with the rest of her life.

*   *   *

Not one minute late, Arline stepped into Stewart Carson's office to keep her long-awaited appointment. She found him hard at work behind his big desk. With her best smile she wished him a cheery good morning.

"Good morning, Arline," he returned, not getting up from his chair. "I must say, you look better this morning than you did last night. It's none of my business, of course. But I'd say you must have put in a hard day yesterday."

"Yes, sir," she smiled. "It was one of the hardest of my life. In more ways than one, I might add."

"Well," Stewart replied, standing up and walking around his desk to shake Arline's hand, "at least Fred Goodson won't be bothering any of us for a while. I don't know what happened to that man. He was a good disc jockey before he slid off the deep end. No matter, though. Everything worked out for the best. I have your contract all drawn up," he said. "But I'd rather you take it with you and have your own attorney look it over before you sign it. That way you'll be certain everything is to your satisfaction. If there's one thing I've learned about doing good business, it's never jump into a deal too quickly. Taking your time up front can often head off regrets at some later time."

Arline knew he was right, of course. "I'm sure I'll find everything in order," she replied, taking the contract from Stewart. "But as you say, this way I'll be even more sure."

"I've worked up a format for the show," Stewart said, handing her a second document. "It's all here in this folder. I'd like to have you look this over, too. I don't know what it is, but something's missing. Your angel gimmick is great, but the show needs something else to set it apart from the run-of-the-mill stuff that's crowding the airways already. Give it some thought, Arline. Perhaps you can come up with something I've missed. I know you're talented in that direction."

Arline glanced at the material in her hand. "I'm not sure I understand, Mr. Carson. Could you be a little more explicit?"

"That's what I'm trying to tell you. I don't know exactly what it is I'm looking for myself. I just know the show needs something to give it that extra spark."

"All right," she agreed. "I'll look it over and give it my best shot."

"Good," Stewart answered crisply, as he began leading Arline toward the door to his office. "I hate to rush you off like this, but I have a staff meeting to organize, and I'm rapidly running out of time. Give me a call when you've had time to consider everything, will you?"

"Yes, sir, I will," she said, stepping through the door and watching it close behind her. "Oh, well," she shrugged after a moment of contemplation. "That's the world of working with Stewart Carson. I'd better get used to it."

That night sleep came more quickly, and this time it was a restful sleep. It would have been even better if the break of dawn hadn't found her wide awake. *What a waste of a Saturday morning,* she thought while standing in the shower much longer than usual. By the time the hands on her clock had reached the nine o'clock mark, she had decided to spend the day doing her favorite thing. She would go shopping. That would take her mind off Bruce. She especially wanted to forget about what he would be doing at high noon.

Funny, she thought. *I don't even know Jenice Anderson, and still I don't like her. Darn if I don't hope Bruce will fail to make that jump. Stop it, Arline! You're acting like a spoiled child. Bruce and Jenice deserve their chance at happiness. Now grow up and let it go, woman!*

One hour and three stores into her shopping spree, Arline stood in front of Casual Corners, looking at a red dress in the window display. Without question she needed a red dress to replace the one destroyed two days earlier. As she admired the dress, her eye caught sight of something else. It was only a reflection in the glass, but it sent chills spiraling up her spine. Instantly she spun to face the person whose reflection she had seen.

"Is it—really you?" she gasped.

"Yes," came the cheerful reply. "It's really me."

"But I thought—I mean—why are you here?"

"What's the matter, Arline? I thought you'd be glad to see me."

"I—I am glad to see you. And I was sure we would see each other again. But I just didn't know it would be this soon."

"I can leave, if you like."

"No! Please don't leave. There's so much I want to say to you."

"Do you remember the last time we saw each other, Arline? It was right here in this mall. In fact, you bought a lovely new green pants suit from this very store."

Tears of joy flooded Arline's eyes, and she was barely able to force the words past the lump that had swelled in her throat. "Oh, yes, I do remember. How could I ever forget such a wonderful day? It was the last time I ever saw you alive—Sam."

CHAPTER SEVENTEEN

"What do you mean Rudolph Pepperdine and his regular pilot aren't here?" Bruce snapped angrily. "I had an appointment for a special jump this morning."

"Yeah, well, somethin' unexpected came up. So yer just gonna hafta settle fer me as yer pilot, I'm afraid."

"But if you're flying the airplane," Bruce argued, "who's going to be in the back to help me with my jump? I've never done this before, and I certainly need someone there to help me."

"Don't worry about it, pal. It's a simple matter of puttin' the plane on automatic pilot long enough ta help ya with the jump. Ya got nothin' ta worry about. Just get in the plane, okay?"

Bruce stared hard at the strange little man standing in front of him. How could Rudolph do this to him? Throwing in a substitute pilot at a time like this was unforgivable. And how could he even think of not being there himself to help with the actual jump? Jumping out of this airplane was going to be tough enough under the best of circumstances. But without Rudolph? Nevertheless, Bruce climbed into the back of the plane.

"This is crazy," Jason argued as Gus took the pilot's seat. "You've never flown an airplane in your life. You'll end up getting Bruce killed, and then you'll be faced with another situation of teaming up a ghost with a living mortal. Do you really want to go through that scenario again?"

"Stop worryin', Jason. Ya know what a multi-talented guy I am. Flyin' this thing is the least of my worries. I could fly it settin' at the desk in my office, if I wanted to. Gettin' Bruce ta jump is the big problem. I mean, it's like we're down for the final count, pal. Either Bruce drops in from the sky and proposes ta the woman today, or it's the Sahara Desert for me. There's no way I'm trustin' Rudolph Pepperdine on this one. I just fixed it so he and his pilot would sleep in a little later than usual this mornin'. What's the big deal?"

Bruce closed the door to the rear compartment of the airplane and strapped himself in. Staring out the little window next to his seat, he pondered the events that had brought him to this frightening point in his life. Thoughts returned to a time when asking the woman he loved to marry him was much less complicated than falling thousands of feet from the sky. For a moment, he was back at the Hunter's Cottage, looking across the dining table into Samantha's lovely face. The memory came so clearly, it was as though he had stepped backward through time to that special evening, the evening she had first agreed to wear his ring. He remembered how she had reacted when she had looked closely at the ring for the first time. It was set with nine stones—five diamonds and four sapphires. The diamond in the center was huge.

"Bruce, I'm not sure I'm ready for this. I still need more time to—"

"I understand," he said, reaching for her hand and gently slipping the ring on her finger. "I promise to be patient, even though patience is not one of my stronger virtues."

"I just don't know," she hesitated, "this ring must have cost you—"

He put two fingers gently against her lips. "The price is not important, darling."

"It is gorgeous," she said at length.

"Then you will wear it?"

"All right, Bruce. I'll wear your ring."

With misty eyes Bruce pulled his safety belt in another notch and latched it tight. Samantha's decision to wear his ring had been the high point of his life up until that time. The happiness he felt that evening was beyond all description. He had known at the time that Samantha was still not a hundred percent ready to accept him as her husband, but he was certain she would do so in time. Shortly after that, Jason Hackett came into his life. What a strange experience it was having a ghost as a rival for the woman he loved!

Moving forward in time, Bruce pictured the trip to his parents' home, where Samantha had apparently come to the decision to go ahead with the marriage plans. She would ask Jason to step out of their lives forever. Nothing could have made Bruce happier. He had won. Or so he thought.

He remembered the last time he saw Samantha alive. It was at the end of a day spent in last-minute preparations for their marriage. He had taken Samantha home to her apartment in the Anderson Building. The wedding was to have been the following day.

"I'll pick you up in the morning, darling, bright and early," Bruce said as he saw Samantha to her door.

"I'd rather you didn't," she replied. *"I'll take a taxi."*

"Why, Samantha? It's no trouble for me to—"

"Bruce, there's something I haven't told you."

"Let me guess. It has something to do with the ghost, am I right?"

"He's coming by in the morning for one last visit. He asked for the chance to say good-bye."

"I thought we were rid of him, once and for all."

"We will be after tomorrow morning. He's given his word."

"I don't like this one bit, Samantha."

"He saved your life, Bruce. You owe him this much."

"Oh, very well, darling," he conceded with a kiss. *"I'll see you in the morning, about ten-thirty."*

As Bruce rode the old elevator to the ground floor, he had no way of knowing the good-night kiss would become a good-bye kiss instead. It was the same elevator that on the following day had taken her away from him forever. How many times had he wished it could have fallen with him inside that evening, instead of waiting one more day.

* * *

"I don't understand how this can be," Arline stammered. "Jason tells me there are rules that must be followed. Why are you here, Sam? And why can I see and hear you?"

"Don't worry, Arline," Samantha quickly assured her friend. "I have the approval of the higher authorities to be here. It took some doing, but with the help of a great friend I managed to sell them on the idea. I'm glad you decided to come to the mall this morning. It's only fitting we share some of our short time together at the same place we last saw each other. Come on, let's go to the food court. Last time you sprang for frozen yogurt. This time is my treat, okay?"

Arline couldn't believe what was happening. It was one thing to be visited by Jason, who came to her as a stranger in the beginning. But Samantha? This was too wonderful to be true. *I must be dreaming,* Arline thought. *Yes, that's it. I'm still at home in bed fast asleep. This is only a dream. A very wonderful dream.*

"I know what you're thinking," Samantha smiled. "If I were in your place, I'd think I was dreaming, too. But I assure you I'm not a dream. I'm very real, and I'm very happy to have the chance to share some time with you again. Even if it will be only a short time."

"I don't suppose I could touch you, just to convince myself you are real?

"Sorry, Arline. I'd give anything for one of your hugs, but—you know the rules."

"The same as with Jason?" Arline asked with a faint smile.

"Exactly the same as Jason," Samantha answered.

"Well, then, I guess I'll just have to settle for seeing you, Sam. You look so alive and beautiful."

"Thanks, Arline. You look pretty good yourself. Now come on, let's go to the food court. Maggie's waiting for us there with a dessert that crazy ghost of mine invented. You're going to love it, I promise."

"Maggie? You mean Gus's secretary?"

"Uh-huh. Maggie and I have become good friends in the time I've been on the other side. She's a sweetheart."

Arline fished a tissue from her purse and wiped her eyes. As the two of them made their way through the mall toward the food court, she asked, "Why did you call Jason a ghost? He's gone to great lengths to convince me he's an angel."

Samantha broke out laughing. "I've been calling him a ghost since the day I first saw him in my old apartment. I love the guy like you can't believe, Arline. But you know me. I have to tease him a little."

Arline joined in with Samantha's laughter. "You haven't changed one bit," she said.

"No, I haven't, Arline. That's part of the beauty of where I live now. We keep our own personalities. It would be tragic if we didn't do that. Hey, look at all those people staring at you; they think you're talking to yourself. This being a ghost is a kick. Jason used to drive me wild when he was playing the part."

Arline glanced up to see. Samantha was right; everyone was look-ing at her. "Oh, well," she replied with a shrug. "If they don't recog-nize me, it doesn't matter. And if they do recognize me, they'll just think this is my angel gimmick that I'm becoming famous for."

"I have to admit," Samantha said. "You're sure taking this better than I did. I was embarrassed to the core."

Arline grinned at her friend. "You've always been too reserved. That's why you had to settle on being a schoolteacher instead of becoming a great television talk show hostess like I'm about to do."

"Too reserved? Just because I don't care for showing off in front of an audience of thousands? I'm a schoolteacher because I like it that way, smarty. And as for your becoming a television celebrity, I hap-pen to have had a little bit to do with that. Keep pushing me, and I may just change my mind and cancel the whole thing."

"You had something to do with my getting the new job? I don't understand."

"Well, to start with, it's something I knew you'd give away your birthday for. And, it's also part of my assignment to get Bruce to the altar, as stipulated in the contract I forced Gus into signing."

"Your assignment? But Jason said—"

"I know what Jason said. He has no idea I even know what's going on here, but he's wrong. Bruce's feelings mean much more to me than they mean to Gus. Like he does with a lot of things, Gus took the matter much too lightly. By the time he realized his computer matchup with Jenice Anderson was in jeopardy, things had gotten badly out of hand. It was then he masterminded this last-ditch effort and enlisted Jason's help. He deliberately tried to keep me in the dark on the whole matter, but fortunately Maggie didn't let that happen. That's when Maggie and I came up with a plan of our own. With her help, we got it past the higher authorities, and—here I am."

Arline stared at her friend. "I'm not sure I understand what you're trying to say, Sam. Jason and I have been working our hearts out with Bruce. We've made great inroads in helping him become the man Jenice wants. Are you telling me we've been wasting our time?"

"Let me answer your question by asking one of my own, Arline. Do you want Jenice to accept Bruce's proposal?"

"Well—I . . ." Arline couldn't answer.

"Hey, this is me you're talking to, remember. Be honest. You'd like to ship Jenice off to Saudi Arabia, wouldn't you?"

"I don't hate Jenice. I just—well, I'm not sure how I do feel about her," Arline concluded reasonably.

Samantha gave a knowing smile. "Come on, admit it. You're jealous of her."

"Why would I be jealous of Jenice Anderson? I have a great new future ahead of me," Arline said loftily.

"What, your television talk show? You and I both know that's not what's foremost on your mind right now. Bruce Vincent holds that place of honor."

"What are you suggesting, Sam? That I'm in love with Bruce myself?"

"Are you?"

Arline stopped cold in her tracks. "I'm not sure," she admitted. "I've never been in love before. I don't know what it's like. How did you know you were in love with Jason?"

Samantha's smile grew three sizes, but she didn't answer Arline's question right away. "Come on," she said. "The food court's just around the corner, and Maggie's there with our goodies."

Samantha bounded off in the direction of the court, leaving her friend to follow her.

"Sometimes I wonder how we ever got to be best friends," Arline said as she caught up with Sam. "You can be a pretty big tease when you want to."

"I work at it," Samantha laughed. "And you know you wouldn't like me any other way."

"You're right," Arline happily agreed. "It just wouldn't be you if that ornery streak ever disappeared." As they rounded the corner, Arline noticed a very attractive woman smiling at them from where she stood near one of the tables. On the table lay two delicious-looking chocolate desserts that looked much like the frozen yogurt Arline liked so well.

"Arline, I'd like you to meet Maggie," Samantha said as they drew near. "Maggie, you already know Arline, of course."

"Yes, Arline," Maggie responded with a nod. "I'm pretty well acquainted with you by this time, thanks to Sam here. You're a lucky woman to have such a good friend on your side."

"I'm happy to meet you, Maggie," Arline smiled. "Jason has told me about you. Thanks for your help with the contest when Fred Goodson was trying to beat me out of my new job."

"You're welcome, I'm sure. The pleasure was all mine. I'm certainly not one of Fred Goodson's fans."

"I couldn't help notice you move the salt and pepper shakers out of the way on the table. Are you . . .?

Maggie smiled and pulled Arline into a warm hug. "I'm at the same level as Gus," she responded cheerfully. "That's why you can feel me now, and it's why I was able to help Sam with the project."

"Let me guess," Arline asked as Maggie stepped away. "It was you who changed the picture Fred was using to blackmail Andrew, wasn't it?"

"It was. I did a pretty good job of computer enhancement, don't you think?"

"Yes, I'd say so. But I'm a little confused. Wasn't that just a tad dishonest, changing the picture to show Fred involved in the bank robbery when it was actually Andrew who drove the car? And shouldn't someone in your position beware of dishonest doings?"

"There's more to the story than you know, Arline. You see, Fred didn't just happen to get that picture of Andrew. It was a setup. Fred is the one who masterminded the bank robbery in the first place. He arranged with the two thugs to trick Andrew into driving the car. All Fred wanted out of the deal was the picture, so he could use it against Andrew whenever he wanted something from the man. So you see, modifying the picture put the blame back where it rightfully belonged. Fred will have a long time to think things over before he ever gets the chance to pull something that conniving again."

Arline was stunned by this information. "Fred did that? Wow, that's an all-time low even for him. It does my heart good to see him get his comeuppance."

"Me, too, Arline," Maggie was quick to agree. "I hate to rush off after meeting you, but duty calls. Gus is due back on the job sometime today after his unexpected trip to the edge of nowhere. You know how men are; they think the office falls apart when they leave for a while."

Arline couldn't help but laugh at this thought. "I don't suppose you have any idea how Gus's invitation to outer space got on the computer in the first place, do you, Maggie?"

"Oh, one never knows," she said slyly, "although actually, it was approved in advance. Samantha convinced the higher authorities she was better able to handle the 'Bruce clause' in the contract than Gus was."

"I'm beginning to smell a cupid here," Arline said, glancing back to Samantha. "The two of you were at the bottom of approving me to be the one Jason worked through, instead of Bruce, right?"

Samantha's smile grew bigger than ever. "I just didn't trust that computer to find a match for Bruce. Especially since I knew Jenice's sister Rebecca. And since you and Bruce were my two best friends—"

"Samantha Allen! I thought you gave up trying to marry me off when we graduated from high school. Now you're at it again. What am I going to do with you?"

"If the two of you will excuse me," Maggie broke in, "I really have to be going."

"It was great meeting you," Arline replied. "Thanks again for everything you've done for me." Then, just like that, Maggie was gone.

Arline shook her head. "I'm telling you, Sam, this dealing with your side takes some getting used to."

"Don't worry, Arline. After today, you won't be bothered with any of us again. Our purpose here will be over, regardless of how this whole thing turns out."

"You mean I'll never see you again?"

"Sure you will—in fifty or so years after you've lived out your normal life on this side. I promise to be the one to come after you when the time is right. Now, sit down and try some of this stuff Jason invented. It's out of this world." She grinned at Arline. "No pun intended."

Arline groaned.

"I swore I'd never do that after putting up with Jason's little quips for so long," Samantha laughed. "But I couldn't resist the opportunity."

Arline took a cautious first bite of the frozen dessert. "This is unbelievable," she exclaimed. "I've never tasted chocolate like this. What is it?"

Samantha shook her head. "I don't have any idea. Jason's the chef of the family. I'm a schoolteacher, remember?"

"Do you still teach school on your side?"

"Almost every day. I've got the greatest bunch of kids in the universe. Especially little Candy Phillips. She reminds me of you when you were young."

Arline took another bite of dessert, and then turned to a more serious subject. "Do you really think I'm in love with Bruce, Sam?"

"Sure you are. It's written all over you."

"But how can I know that for myself? You never did answer my question of how you knew you were in love with Jason."

Samantha took a bite of her own dessert and allowed her mind to drift back to the time she was being courted by her wonderful ghost. "I knew I was in love when I couldn't think of anything else but him. And when life lost all its meaning at the thought of not having him around. And you know, even after I understood my own heart, I almost made a terrible mistake. I knew I could never love Bruce the way I loved Jason, but I didn't have the faith that life could offer us anything more than what we had at the time. I thought a natural life with Bruce would be better than an unnatural life with a ghost. How wrong I was, Arline. I've never been as happy as I am now."

Arline smiled in understanding. "I have to admit, Jason is special. I remember how confused I was when you first tried to tell me you were in love with a ghost. You have to realize that was a little strange to me at the time."

Samantha dropped her spoon to the edge of her dish. "Let me ask you another question, Arline. How did it make you feel when you learned about being selected for your new job?"

"I think you already know the answer to that question. You must have been somewhere around, watching me when it happened. It was the greatest thrill of my life."

"I'm sure it was. But how do you feel about it right now?"

Arline thought a moment before answering. "It just doesn't seem as exciting or important as it did three weeks ago."

"That's because you have something else pressing on your mind. You and I both know what that something else is, don't we, Arline?"

"Yes," she sighed. "It's Bruce."

"Admit it, woman, you're in love with him. Whatever you do, don't make the same mistake I almost made. Go to him, and tell him how you feel."

Arline's eyes glistened. "I can't, Sam. He's going to jump from an airplane in just over an hour. When he lands on Howard Placard's beach, he's going to ask Jenice Anderson to be his wife."

"So, you plan to just sit here and let that happen without putting up a fight for the man you love?"

"What can I do?"

"You can jump in that Toyota of yours and get to that beach while there's still time. When Bruce lands, he can find two choices waiting for him. I know Bruce, Arline. I know him better than his own mother knows him. You're the one he's in love with. He may not even know it right now, but it's the truth, nevertheless."

"Do you really think I should go to the beach?"

"I haven't gone to all the trouble of giving the two of you the chance to fall in love for nothing. Now, finish that dessert and go get in your car."

* * *

Bruce glanced at his watch. It eleven-thirty. *Why are you doing this, Bruce Vincent?* he asked himself. *You know you're not in love with Jenice Anderson. You never have been. You merely grabbed for the first brass ring you spotted after losing Samantha. Why not just let her walk out of your life? Why are you putting yourself through the torture of making this jump?*

Just as he was about to convince himself to leave the airplane, he felt it lurch into motion. And—it was too late.

CHAPTER EIGHTEEN

It was a quarter of noon when Arline pulled up to the guard shack at Howard Placard's beach. "Hello, Miss Wilson," the security guard said as she rolled down her window to identify herself. He recognized her from the evening she and Bruce had come to the beach to fly their kite.

"Hi, Ralph," Arline greeted him.

"Are you here to see the show, too?" he asked.

"What show?" she asked curiously. "You mean, Bruce's parachute jump onto the beach?"

"Yes, ma'am, that's what I mean." He nodded his head. "Ms. Anderson is already here. She doesn't think Bruce will actually do it. From my experience with him, I'd have to agree with her."

"Well, both you and Ms. Anderson are wrong," Arline protested. "Bruce Vincent is one of the bravest men I've ever known. He'll jump out of that plane, you just wait and see."

Ralph looked abashed. "To tell you the truth, I hope you're right. Bruce and I go way back. I can't think of a better way for him to improve his self-image than by taking up the hobby of skydiving. I wouldn't even mind losing our little agreement over his planned adventure. You see, if he makes the jump on schedule, I have to roll up his parachute and hold onto it until his instructor picks it up later. If he fails to make the jump, he owes me a steak dinner."

"I tell you what I'll do, Ralph. If this turns out with you having to pack up that chute, I'll see to it you're invited as a guest on one of my first television shows to tell the world about his jump. Do we have a deal?"

"Television show?" Ralph asked. "I thought your show was on the radio, Ms. Wilson."

"Not any more it's not. Starting next month, I'm the hostess of a new televised talk show. Now, how about it? If Bruce makes the jump, will you appear as a guest on my show?"

Ralph smiled and pointed toward the parking lot. "You can park over there in the lot next to Ms. Anderson's Jeep. Have a nice day, ma'am, but don't be too disappointed if Bruce stands you up."

"You didn't answer my question, Ralph."

"I'll make you the same offer I made Bruce. If it turns out I don't have to roll up that parachute, you owe me a steak dinner, too. If by some chance I find I've misjudged the man, and he does go through with it, I'll be glad to appear on your television show. It would do my heart good to tell the world about Bruce Vincent jumping out of an airplane."

"You're on, Ralph," Arline said with a thumbs-up sign as she pulled forward into the parking lot.

After parking her car, she stepped out and searched the beach for signs of Jenice. She finally spotted her several yards away, sitting on a large rock. Even though Arline had never met Jenice, she recognized her immediately from the picture Bruce carried in his wallet.

"There she is, Sam," Arline said, pointing in Jenice's direction. "I don't know which would be better—introduce myself or wait here until Bruce drops in."

"Let's go meet the woman," Samantha insisted, as she started off in the direction of the rock where Jenice was seated. "It's always better to know everything you can about your competition."

"I suppose you're right," Arline agreed, trying to catch up. "You will stay close to me though, won't you? Come to think of it, why isn't Jason here? Where is he, anyway?"

"Jason and Gus are in the plane with Bruce. They're in for the shock of their life when they find me here with you, Arline. They both still think this project is in their hands."

"Jason doesn't know you're here with me, then?" Arline asked.

"No way," Samantha laughed. "Those two think they're the brains behind all this. I can't wait to see their faces when they find me here and learn what I've been up to."

"Your mean streak is showing again, Sam."

Samantha grinned. "Yes, and I intend to enjoy every second of my little surprise."

By this time they had almost reached the rock where Jenice was seated.

"Would you look at her, Sam?" Arline gulped. "She's even more beautiful than her picture. No wonder Bruce has gone to so much trouble trying to please her. I think I'm in trouble."

"Don't be ridiculous, Arline. You're much prettier than she is. And knowing both you and Bruce the way I do, I can guarantee you're in first place in his book."

"Hi," Arline said, forcing a smile. "You must be Jenice Anderson." Arline cringed at the sickening sweetness in her own voice.

"Yes, I'm Jenice," came the cautious reply. "But I'm afraid you have me at a disadvantage. Should I know you?"

"No, we've never met. My name's Arline Wilson. I'm a good friend of Bruce."

"Arline Wilson? You're the disc jockey who claims to talk with an angel, right?"

Anger rolled up Arline's neck at the words "disc jockey," but she bit her tongue and tried to ignore the remark. "One and the same. Have you heard my show?"

"Not for the last few weeks. But I used to listen to you regularly. You're a very talented woman, Arline, and I enjoy the variety of music your station plays. How do you know Bruce?"

"Bruce and I have been good friends for a very long time. He came to me for help when you gave him the challenge of jumping from the plane."

A puzzled look crossed Jenice's face as she studied Arline care-fullly. "Why?" she asked.

"Why what?" Arline returned.

"Why would Bruce ask your help to learn skydiving? Is it a hobby of yours, or something?"

Arline felt the hair on the back of her neck bristle. She had a definite feeling she was being backed into a corner, and she didn't like it. Quickly evaluating the situation, she concluded that the only way to deal with Jenice was to meet her head-on with the truth.

"Actually, Jenice," she said matter-of-factly, "it wasn't Bruce's idea to come to me for help. It was my angel's idea. I only agreed to help out as a favor to the angel."

Jenice lifted her eyebrows. "Your angel asked you to help Bruce learn to skydive? I think there's more here than you're letting on, Ms. Wilson. Perhaps your interest in Bruce is somehow connected with your radio talk show?"

Arline shook her head. "No. My career has nothing to do with my interest in Bruce."

"If that's true, then why tie the angel to your association with him? Wait." Jenice narrowed her eyes speculatively. "I think I can answer my own question. You have eyes for Bruce yourself, don't you?"

Arline was taken aback by Jenice's boldness, but she answered honestly. "I'd be lying if I denied that. But believe what you may, I only want what's best for Bruce. If that means stepping aside and letting him be part of your life, then so be it. But one thing I have to know before I can do that: are you really in love with him?"

"Am I in love with Bruce?" Jenice cocked her head to the side. "That's a little bit personal, wouldn't you say?"

"Yes, it is personal," Arline agreed calmly. "But I don't want to see him hurt. I find it hard to believe you could give him an ultimatum like this skydiving thing if you really love him."

Jenice smiled ruefully. "I give you my word, Ms. Wilson, the last thing I want to do is hurt Bruce. To the contrary, I'm trying my best to spare his feelings."

"Trying to spare his feelings?" Arline asked sharply. "Why did you ever accept his ring in the first place if you didn't love him enough to be his wife? I'm sorry, but it doesn't sound like you're trying to spare his feelings at all."

Jenice rose from the rock where she had been sitting and walked over next to Arline. "You're in love with Bruce, aren't you?" she asked bluntly. "That's why you're so protective of him, isn't it?"

"Yes!" Arline snapped. "I admit it. I am in love with Bruce. But I do want what's best for him even if that means giving him up to you."

Jenice reached down and picked up a sea shell from the sand near her feet. For several seconds she studied the shell. "Do you mind if I call you Arline?" she finally asked.

"Actually, I'd prefer that."

Looking up from the shell, Jenice let her eyes meet Arline's. "Let me explain some things to you," she began. "I first met Bruce at the funeral of a previous fiancée. Her name was Samantha Allen. I'm sure you must have known Samantha, if you're a longtime friend of Bruce."

"I knew Sam," Arline quickly came back. *Still do, as a matter of fact,* she thought, with a glance in Samantha's direction.

Jenice nodded and went on with her explanation. "My sister Rebecca pushed Bruce and me together from the first. Bruce was heartsick at the time and needed a friend. I decided that perhaps I could help him. After all, Bruce is an attractive man. But it took only a few dates to realize Bruce was not my type. Still, he was pleasant to be with.

"In the beginning it was my sister Rebecca who insisted I keep seeing him, but I have to admit that after a while I actually came to like Bruce. The major problem proved to be the difference in our lifestyles. Bruce is an easygoing, stay-at-home sort of man. I'm an adventuress. In time it became evident I would have to choose between Bruce and my lifetime dream to go exploring. The choice wasn't an easy one, Arline.

"In the end I decided to hold on to my dream. I manufactured this skydiving scheme because I know Bruce well enough to know he could never go through with it. Instead of breaking off cold with him, I gave him a month to get used to the idea. At the same time I gave him the chance to see how impossible our relationship would be. Surely it's obvious to him by this time that the two of us are not compatible. If he can't parachute out of an airplane, how could he do the things I want from a husband?

"You ask me if I love him. Yes, I do. Like you, I want the best for him. And I'm sure that isn't me."

Reaching for Arline's hand, Jenice slid the sea shell she had been holding into it. "This shell," she said, "is very beautiful. I'm sure you're the sort of woman to enjoy its beauty. Unfortunately, I'm not one to enjoy it unless the creature is still alive to offer me the adventure of capturing it. The way it is now, I only had to reach to my feet and pick it up. I give you the shell, Arline. And I give you Bruce, as well. Both are very wonderful in their own way. Hold them close to your heart, and be happy."

Arline stared at the shell in her hand. "I—I'm sorry," she said at last. "It seems I've misjudged you. What can I say?"

"You don't need to say anything, Arline. In another ten minutes the field will be wide open to you. I'm sure Bruce won't be able to bring himself to jump from the plane. That will give me the opportunity to just disappear from his life. One thing I would like to ask, Arline. Please, don't tell Bruce I couldn't have gone through with the marriage even if he had made the jump. I don't want him to go on loving me, but I can't stand the idea of him thinking badly of me."

"You have my word, Jenice," Arline promised. "But I think you're wrong about Bruce not making the jump. If I were a betting person, I'd put a bundle on him showing up here on time."

"You are in love with Bruce, aren't you?" Jenice smiled. "I hope you do manage to bring him around. I'm sure you'll be good for him."

Arline stared speechless at this woman she wanted so much to resent but couldn't. One by one Jenice had dismantled each of Arline's arguments. As she pondered what to say next, her thoughts were scattered by the sound of a familiar, and perturbed, voice.

"Sam?! What are you doing here?!"

Arline spun to see Jason, wide-eyed and mouth hanging open, standing next to Samantha. "I wondered when you'd show up," Samantha said, sliding her arms around Jason's neck and giving him a big kiss. "You sure took your own sweet time getting here."

"But—why are you here, Sam? Gus told me . . ."

"Gus told you what?" she teased.

"He told me—that is, he said . . ."

"He told you I didn't know anything about what the two of you have been up to the last month."

"But how—"

"Jason Hackett!" Samantha scolded. "You should know by now you can't put anything over on me. And another thing," she said, gently stroking his hair with one hand. "This playing ghost isn't nearly as bad as you always tried to make me believe. As a matter of fact,

I'm enjoying every minute of it. Don't you ever try to play on my sympathy again because you spent twenty years doing it."

Jason's face showed his confusion. "Sam, cut it out and tell me what's going on. You're going to be in deep trouble with the higher authorities for coming here without their approval."

"For your information, Mr. Hackett, I have their approval. I've been conducting this project from the beginning. I only let you think Gus was still in charge because you deserved it. The two of you plotted to keep me in the dark, didn't you?"

"That was Gus's idea, not mine. I wanted to tell you everything from the first," Jason defended himself.

"I know that, too." Samantha leaned forward to kiss Jason's cheek. "That's why you're not in real trouble with me. But you see, I couldn't trust you and Gus to tinker with the lives of my two best friends here on this side. So I had to become personally involved."

"Well, thanks for the vote of confidence," Jason grumbled. "But you didn't need to get involved. Bruce is on his way here right now to propose to Jenice. If you listen carefully, you can hear the sound of the plane. Which, by the way, Gus is flying. The two of us aren't exactly helpless, you know."

"Jason, Jason," she sighed. "I can't believe how blind you can be at times. How do you think Arline would feel if Bruce proposes to Jenice?"

Jason looked at her blankly. "How do I think Arline would feel? She'd feel great. After all the work she's done to get these two together, how is she supposed to feel?"

Samantha smiled at him tolerantly. "I admit you're the greatest chef I've ever known, my funny little ghost. But as a cupid you just struck out. It's Arline that we have to get Bruce to propose to. Look at her, Jason. Surely even you can see she's the one in love with Bruce."

Jason broke into laughter. "Arline in love with Bruce? That's preposterous." Then turning to Arline, Jason said, "You must think I'm crazy carrying on like this. I know you can't see her, but Sam's here. She's standing right beside me. I give you my word, Arline, I haven't been arguing with myself."

"I know Sam's here, Jason," Arline said, watching Jenice's reaction out of the corner of her eye. "I can see her. And she's right about Bruce. I am in love with him."

"You're talking to your angel again?" Jenice asked.

"I'm talking to two of them this time," Arline grinned. "Sounds crazy, doesn't it?"

"Well," Jenice answered. "I suppose it's all part of your profession. It does sound a little crazy, though."

"What do you mean you're in love with Bruce?" Jason demanded. "The contract clearly states that he has to marry Jenice Anderson. And how the heck can you see Sam? That's against the rules."

"It's not against the rules, Jason," Samantha explained. "The higher authorities make the rules. They can do whatever they like. And concerning the contract, I'm the one who wrote it. Nowhere does it stipulate that Bruce has to marry Jenice Anderson. I only required him to be married within a year of the time the contract was signed. If he marries Arline, the contract is completely satisfied, and so am I."

"Wait a minute," Arline protested. "What about me? Since we're talking about my future here, shouldn't I have some say in whether or not I marry Bruce?"

"This is more than just a gimmick, isn't it?" Jenice asked, a worried crease in her forehead. "You really do believe you're talking to these angels, don't you?"

"This makes no sense at all, Arline," Jason pressed. "If you're in love with Bruce, why did you go to all the trouble to help him become the man Jenice wants?"

Arline shot a frustrated look at Jenice. "I am talking to angels, Jenice. And right now I'm ready to shoot one of them if he doesn't shut up."

"Look!" Samantha cried, pointing toward the sky. "It's a parachute. Bruce did it! He actually made the jump."

Arline glanced skyward. "It is Bruce!" she shouted. "Look, Jenice! I told you he'd do it, didn't I. Now what do you think of Bruce?"

Jenice appeared dumbstruck. "It seems you know the man much better than I do. I have to hand it to you, Arline. Whatever you did to convince him to go through with this stunt was more than I could have done."

* * *

Bruce had never been so terrified in his entire life. *Who was flying the plane when that strange little man came to the back compartment and shoved me out? I can't believe this is happening. And why are there two women down there on the beach?* In desperation, he fought to remember everything Rudolph Pepperdine had taught him about guiding the chute. To his great relief, it worked. He found himself headed for a landing in the soft sand not more than twenty-five feet from where the two women were waiting. As he came closer, he was shocked to see the second woman on the beach was Arline.

"Arline!" he shouted. "You changed your mind and came to see me jump after all."

A knot the size of a lemon formed in the pit of Bruce's stomach as the ground rushed swiftly toward him. Taking a deep breath and bending his knees as Rudolph had directed, he hit the turf and rolled into a ball on the soft sand. In an instant, it was over.

"I'm alive," he exulted. "I did it, and I'm still alive!"

By the time he looked up, both Jenice and Arline were standing over him with worried looks.

"I did it," he managed to say, with a big smile showing through a face full of sand. "I really did it, didn't I?"

CHAPTER NINETEEN

Arline fell to the sand beside Bruce. "Are you all right?" she shouted, brushing the sand from his hair with her fingers.

"Yes, I am all right," he answered happily. "I did it, Arline, and I'm all right."

"Thank heaven," she sighed. Then she realized that it was Jenice for whom he had done the act, not for her. At this thought she slowly rose to her feet and stood back out of the way.

Bruce stood to remove the harness, then brushed the sand off himself. He stepped directly in front of Jenice and placed one hand on her shoulder. "You look lovely, my dear. A little surprised, perhaps, but lovely nevertheless."

"Yes, Bruce," she answered honestly. "I am surprised. I admit, I didn't think you could do it."

"Well to be perfectly honest, I'm still not sure I could have done it myself. Much as I hate to admit it, I was pushed."

"Pushed?" Jenice puzzled. "But who would have pushed you? Was it your instructor?"

"No, it wasn't Rudolph. I suspect it was an angel named Gus. I've never seen him before this morning, but he looked exactly as I've pictured him for some time now."

"You're talking to angels, too? That's another side of you I've never seen before. First, you show nerve enough to parachute from a plane, and now you tell me you talk to angels."

"Well, I'm not actually sure the guy who pushed me was Gus," Bruce admitted. "And then again, I'm not sure the real Gus could be called an angel. But I am sure there's one angel close by who goes by the name of Jason. Much as I'd like to say I've spoken to him personally, I can't. Arline's the only one who has that privilege. Speaking of

Arline," he said, turning to her. "What made you change your mind about being here to see me jump?"

Arline lowered her eyes so she was not looking directly at Bruce. "I shouldn't have come," she replied. "I let an angel talk me into it."

"I'm glad Jason talked you into coming. After all we've been through together, I'd like you to hear what I have to say to Jenice."

Arline wanted to explain it wasn't Jason who talked her into being at the beach, but before she could say anything, Bruce pulled a little black ring box from his trouser pocket. He opened it and Arline thought her heart would break as she listened to what he said next.

"Jenice, exactly one month ago you returned my ring. You said you would only accept it again if I could prove myself. You wanted to know for sure I could make some changes in my lifestyle. Changes that would make me a more exciting man and one you could spend a lifetime with."

"Yes, Bruce, what you say is true. But—"

"Please, Jenice, let me finish. I want you to look closely at the ring in this box. You'll notice, it's not the same ring you returned to me. This is the ring Samantha once wore. You see, this last month has done more than just change my attitude about my lifestyle. It's given me a chance to take a close look at what Bruce Vincent is really all about. For the first time I realize just how deeply in love with Samantha I was. This ring has been safely tucked away ever since I lost her, and I vowed never to let it be worn by another.

"But something has happened to change my mind. I've fallen in love again, Jenice, and I want my new love to accept this ring as proof that my feelings for her go even beyond those I once felt for Samantha. Does that make sense to you?"

"Bruce," Jenice said, gently folding his hand closed around the little box. "I can't accept the ring from you. Please try to understand. I don't want to hurt you, but I just can't accept it."

"No, Jenice," Bruce explained, also trying hard to be gentle. "You don't understand. I know now the two of us could never be happy together. I'm sure you know it, too. This ring," he said, turning slowly to face Arline, "is for the love I found in a lady who saw something in me no one else could. You are the one I'm offering the ring to, Arline, and my heart goes with it."

Arline gasped. "Are you asking me to marry you?" Her knees started to quiver.

"I am, if you'll have me," he said humbly.

"If I'll have you!" she cried, throwing herself into his open arms with a force that sent the two of them tumbling to the soft sand. The kiss she pressed to his lips left no doubt in his mind, or in anyone else's, she was in love with him. And the pride she felt for the courage he had shown in jumping from the plane earned him a second kiss, no less passionate than the first.

"Can I take that as a yes?" Bruce asked, once she let him catch his breath.

"You can take that as a *resounding* yes," she said, poking a finger to the end of his nose. "I've never felt for a man what I feel for you, Bruce. I'm in love and I love the feeling. It's like nothing I've ever experienced before."

"Better even than when you learned about your new job?" he asked.

Arline faked a frown. "Boy," she teased. "That's a tough one. Let me think about it a while, okay?"

"You better not have to think about it," Bruce growled, forcing her against the sand with a kiss of his own.

"Okay," she admitted with a twinkle in her eye. "Better even than getting my new job." Glancing up at Jason and Samantha, Arline started to laugh. Samantha was all smiles, while Jason looked shocked.

"Now what are you laughing at?" Bruce asked, noticing Arline's attention had turned away from him. "Is Jason telling you you're making a big mistake, marrying a wimp like me?"

"No, Bruce," she answered. "Jason's not saying a word. But there's something I think you should know. Jason's not alone. There's another angel standing right beside him."

"You mean Gus?" Bruce asked, rolling over and looking where he supposed Jason to be.

"No, I don't mean Gus. This angel is much prettier than him, I assure you."

"What! Are you saying—"

"Yes, Bruce. Sam's here. And I've been allowed to see her, too."

A look of astonishment filled Bruce's face, and he fell speechless.

"Excuse me," Jenice spoke up. "I really don't know what's going on here, but it's obvious I'm no longer a part of it. I wish you both the best of luck. You deserve it." As she walked away, she added lightly, "You might name your first daughter after me."

"Make it my second and you have a deal," Arline replied with a smile. "My first daughter is going to be named Samantha."

Jenice waved and returned to her car, and it was with bittersweet emotion that Arline and Bruce watched her drive out of their lives forever.

"Samantha?" Bruce said, when Jenice had gone. "I can neither see nor hear you, but I do believe you're here. I want you to know that losing you was the hardest mountain I've ever had to climb. But I also know now that I'm not the one you were in love with. I've come to know Jason pretty well these last few weeks, and I must say you have a great guy there. I'm sure the two of you are happy, and I'm just as sure I can be happy, too. Now that I've found Arline, that is."

"Tell him thanks, Arline," Samantha said. "And tell him I wish the two of you all the luck in the world."

Arline squeezed Bruce's hand. "Sam said to say thanks, Bruce. And she wishes us luck. But before I accept the ring from you, I have to ask Sam how she feels about my wearing it. After all, it was her ring. How about it, Sam? Do you mind my wearing the ring you once wore?"

"Of course I don't mind, Arline. The question is, how do you feel about it?"

"How do I feel? This ring will bring me happiness the rest of my life. Not only will it be the symbol of my love for Bruce, it will be a reminder of how close you are to me as well. I can think of nothing that would please me more."

Bruce pulled Arline to him and would have kissed her, but he was interrupted by a familiar voice.

"Well, now, isn't this a cozy little bunch. I'm probably gonna be sorry fer askin', but what are you doin' here, Sam?"

"It's you again!" Bruce cried when he spotted Gus. "How did you get here so fast? Who's flying the airplane?"

"Flyin' the plane is no problem, pal. But the way I see it, we have a problem here. Wasn't that Jenice I just saw headin' fer the hills in the brown Jeep?"

"It was Jenice," Samantha answered. "And that's what I'm doing here—making sure you and Jason don't muddy the waters. Bruce has just proposed to Arline, so we no longer need Jenice."

"You are Gus, aren't you?" Bruce asked excitedly. "That's how you managed to get here from the plane, and why you're not worried about how it's flying."

"Ya got that one right, Bruce. On both counts. Now, what's this bit about you proposin' ta' Arline? You were supposed ta propose to Jenice. If this ain't a kettle of worms, I never saw one."

"Kettle of worms?" Bruce asked. "Don't you mean can of worms?"

"It's all right, Gus," Samantha assured him. "If Bruce marries Arline, your contract will be closed out with honors. You and Jason never read it close enough to realize it makes no difference who Bruce marries, just so long as he marries within the time specified. The man loves Arline, and she loves him. Now back off, and let well enough alone, will you?"

"Whaddya mean back off? This is my project, ya know. What are you doin' here pokin' around anyhow?"

"I'm saving your hide, Gus. That's what I'm doing. Just count your blessings that if you ever see the Sahara Desert, it will be as nothing more than a tourist."

"I—don't suppose," Bruce asked hesitantly, "there's any way I could be allowed to see Samantha, is there? I'd give anything to see her just once more."

"I don't know," Gus replied cautiously. "I might be persuaded ta stick my neck out for ya. Are you tellin' me the truth, Sam? If Bruce marries Arline, am I off the hook on the contract?"

"I'm telling you the truth, Gus."

"There's somethin' ya gotta understand, Bruce. Bendin' the rule far enough ta let ya see Sam would cost me a bundle. I have a friend in the right place ta justify it for me, but this guy will expect a payback big enough ta choke a mule. I'll consider lettin' ya' see her on one condition. Ya gotta give me yer word ta get Arline in that weddin' dress before the deadline."

"You have my word, Gus," Bruce said with no hesitation. "You'll have to clue me in on the date of the deadline, though. I have no idea when or what it is."

"You have my word, too, Gus," Samantha added. "And I promise not to give you any more trouble over your trying to keep me in the dark on the project."

"That last part does the trick for sure, Sam. Ya got a deal. And just because I'm all heart, I'll even throw Jason in with the bargain. Take a good look, Bruce. You're about ta see yerself a couple of angels."

Bruce watched in awe as the two figures began to materialize before his eyes. At first they appeared transparent, like the reflection from a glass window. But within seconds, he saw them as clearly as life itself.

"Samantha," he said, his voice barely a whisper. "You look so lovely. I have no question about your happiness. It shines like a brilliant summer sunrise."

"Thank you, Bruce. I must say, you look pretty good, yourself. Arline's done wonders with you."

Bruce turned to Jason. "So you're Jason Hackett? I wish I could shake your hand. I've come to know what a good friend you are to me these last few weeks."

"Ditto, Bruce. You're an all-right guy, yourself. I'm sorry I ever called you a wimp. That was a nice landing you made, by the way. I was in the army long enough to see plenty of parachutists do their thing, and I never saw one land any better than you did."

"You can really see them?" Arline asked.

Bruce squeezed her hand. "Yes, Arline, I can see them."

"I think we'd better be careful who we tell about this," she laughed, giving him a push to the shoulder. "It might not be the best advertisement for your profession."

"Okay, okay," Gus interrupted. "Enough of this mushy stuff. It's time ya let me know how this all happened. Sam, I know you couldn't have handled it by yerself. Who did ya get to help ya?"

"It was Maggie," Samantha explained. "She helped me get permission from the higher authorities to get the ball rolling. Then she pulled a few strings to keep it in motion."

"Yeah? Well, that figures," Gus grumbled, though he admitted with a grin, "Ya know darn well I could never be mad at Maggie. And I have ta admit, everythin' came up tulips in the end."

"Roses, Gus," Arline chuckled. "The saying is 'Everything came up roses.'"

"Whatever," he said with a casual wave of his hand. "Ya know what I mean."

"Oh, Samantha," Bruce sighed. "I'm so glad I was allowed to see you. Now that I've seen how happy you are with Jason, it certainly makes getting on with my life easier."

"I'd say having Arline close to you will help in that department, too," Samantha teased. "Say hello to your mother for me, will you? I love her almost as much as you do."

"We won't be seeing either of you again, will we?" Arline asked sadly.

"I told you before, Arline. When it comes your time, in another fifty years or so, I'll be here to get you. And I promise to take you shopping in a few malls like you've never imagined."

"You have shopping malls over there?"

"You know me. I'd go crazy if they didn't have malls."

"Jason," Bruce said, after clearing his throat. "I never did get the chance to thank you for saving my life that time."

"Think nothing of it, Bruce. You just take good care of Arline. If you don't, I just might be back to haunt you."

Bruce laughed. "I'd say it's a little too late for that. You may have given me a few frights in the past, but I know you better now. I will take good care of Arline, though. Just as I'm sure you'll take good care of Sam."

"You called me Sam," Samantha laughed. "I never heard you do that before."

"You're right. But somehow Sam seems to fit you now. I suppose it goes along with some of my other changes."

"I hate ta be the one ta bring this up," Gus said. "But lettin' these two angels remain visible is costin' me by the second. How about closin' it down, okay?"

"All right," Samantha sighed. "It looks like everything is in order now. Thanks for being a sport, Gus."

"Think nothin' of it, Sam. I'll see ya on the other side. But make it snappy, okay? I'm in pretty deep as it is already." With this, Gus turned and started walking away.

As Arline watched, she was amazed to see him vanish after only a few steps.

"Well, you two angels," she said looking back to Samantha and Jason. "I guess this is good-bye, at least for now. I wish I could hug you both, but . . ."

"Good-bye, Arline," Jason said. "It's been a thrill a minute."

"It certainly has." Arline smiled at him, despite the tear that trickled from the corner of her eye. "I'll never forget you." Then, turning to Samantha, she added, "You know I'll never forget you either, Sam. I'm holding you to your word on the shopping trip in fifty or so years."

"Good-bye, Arline," Samantha said, smiling. "Have a wonderful life."

It took a moment or so for Arline to get her voice back. When she did, she said, "I want you both to know how much I love and appreciate you. Thanks for giving me the best gift I've ever had."

"That goes for me, too," Bruce said, taking Arline by the arm and pulling her close. "I hope you weren't joking when you said you liked the idea of opening up the old Henderson Lodge and railroad line. Because that's exactly what I plan on doing. I signed the papers yesterday. I now own the whole business. Lodge, railroad, everything. Elmo came along with the deal, of course."

"Oh, Bruce!" Arline cried. "How exciting! I love the idea, except . . ." Arline's smile faded as her shoulders fell into a slump.

"Except for your television show?" Bruce asked.

"Yes," she sighed. "How could I do a show five days every week and still live up the mountain with you? I guess this means giving up my dream of being a talk show hostess."

"No it doesn't," Bruce said, brushing back her hair with his hand. "You see, when I made up my mind yesterday to ask you to marry me, I took the liberty of talking to Stewart Carson. I suggested we set up a television studio right at the lodge. I even agreed to put all the guests up in one of our best suites at no charge. The man was ecstatic. He loved the idea and couldn't quit raving about how it was exactly the answer to what had been missing from the format. All you have to do is sign the contract, and the deal is cast in stone."

Arline shrieked with joy and pulled Bruce to her in another lingering kiss. "I can't believe this!" she murmured when their lips parted. "I'm getting a dream husband and a dream job at the same time. How could life get any better than this?"

Turning back to where Samantha and Jason had been standing, Arline discovered they were gone.

"I guess it's just you and me now," she said sliding an arm through Bruce's. "What do you say we get on with our lives, darling?"

"That's supposed to be my line," Bruce laughed. Then, after one final look at where he had last seen Samantha, he led the way back toward Arline's car.

For the record, Jenice Anderson never did go on an African safari. Arline and Bruce did, however. On the tenth anniversary of their marriage.

ABOUT THE AUTHOR

Dan Yates has always enjoyed writing. "I've spent most of my working career doing technical writing in one form or another," he says. "Now in the shadow of my retirement years, I'm trying something new. I'd like to thank Covenant Communications for giving my stories the chance to be told." A former bishop and high councilman, Dan is employed by Arizona Public Service Company.

Dan's writing efforts have resulted in Church productions and local publications, as well as his best-selling novel, *Angels Don't Knock*.

Dan and his wife, Shelby Jean, live in Phoenix, Arizona. They have six children and sixteen grandchildren.

Dan would love to hear from his readers. You can write to him at:

3434 W. Greenway #26-285
Phoenix, AZ 85023